Air Force Enlisted Careers & Job Opportunities

A GUIDE TO AIR FORCE SPECIALTY CODES
(AFSC)

Lawrence Keith

Copyright © 2018 by Lawrence Keith

Most all information provided in this book was gathered through Air Force, Department of Defense, and other United States government regulations and policies. The information provided in this book was current at the time of publishing. All information gathered was compiled and presented in this book for your enjoyment.

All rights reserved. No part of this book may be reproduced or used in any form without written permission from the publisher.

Air Force Enlisted Careers & Job Opportunities: A Guide to Air Force Specialty Codes (AFSC) / Lawrence Keith – 1st Edition.
ISBN 978-1726030663

Cover Design: Lawrence Keith
Cover photo obtained from AF.mil, and is considered public information according to the Overview paragraph on the Disclaimer webpage.
Cover Photo Credit: SrA Kathryn Reaves

Contents

Air Crew Operations Careers (1A) 1
   1A0X1 In-Flight Refueling 3
   1A2X1 Aircraft Loadmaster 5
   1A3X1 Airborne Mission Systems Operator 7
   1A8X1 Airborne Cryptologic Language Analyst 9
   1A8X2 Airborne Intelligence, Surveillance and Reconnaissance (ISR) Operator 11
   1A9X1 Special Missions Aviation 13

Command and Control Systems Operations Careers (1C) 15
   1C0X2 Aviation Resource Management 17
   1C1X1 Air Traffic Control 19
   1C2X1 Combat Control 21
   1C3X1 Command and Control Operations 23
   1C4X1 Tactical Air Control Party Specialist 25
   1C5X1 Command and Control Battle Management Operations 27
   1C6X1 Space Systems Operations 29
   1C7X1 Airfield Management 31
   1C8X3 Radar, Airfield, & Weather Systems (RAWS) 33

Intelligence Careers (1N) 35
   1N0X1 Operations Intelligence 37
   1N1X1 Geospatial Intelligence 39
   1N2X1 Signals Intelligence Analyst 41
   1N3X1 Cryptologic Language Analyst 43
   1N4X1 Fusion Analyst 45

Aircrew Flight Equipment Careers (1P) 47

1P0X1 Aircrew Flight Equipment..49

Aircrew Protection Careers (1T) 51

    1T0X1 Survival, Evasion, Resistance and Escape (SERE).........................53

    1T2X1 Pararescue..55

Remotely Piloted Aircraft Sensor Operator Careers (1U).................................57

    1U0X1 Remotely Piloted Aircraft (RPA) Sensor Operator 59

Weather Careers (1W) 61

    1W0X1 Weather 63

    1W0X2 Special Operations Weather Technician 65

Aerospace Maintenance Careers (2A) 67

    2A0X1 Avionics Test Station and Components 69

    2A2X1 Special Operations Forces/Personnel Recovery (SOF/PR) Integrated Communication / Navigation / Mission Systems.....................71

    2A2X2 Special Operations Forces/Personnel Recovery (SOF/PR) Integrated Instrument and Flight Control Systems.....................................73

    2A2X3 Special Operations Forces/Personnel Recovery (SOF/PR) Integrated Electronic Warfare Systems..75

    2A3X3 Tactical Aircraft Maintenance..77

    2A3X4 Fighter Aircraft Integrated Avionics 79

    2A3X5 Advanced Fighter Aircraft Integrated Avionics..............................81

    2A3X7 Tactical Aircraft Maintenance (5th Generation) 82

    2A3X8 Remotely Piloted Aircraft Maintenance 83

    2A5X1 Airlift / Special Mission Aircraft Maintenance...............................85

    2A5X2 Helicopter / Tiltrotor Aircraft Maintenance 87

    2A5X3 Mobility Air Forces Electronic Warfare Systems...........................89

    2A5X4 Refuel / Bomber Aircraft Maintenance 91

    2A6X1 Aerospace Propulsion..93

2A6X2 Aerospace Ground Equipment 95

2A6X3 Aircrew Egress Systems 97

2A6X4 Aircraft Fuel Systems 99

2A6X5 Aircraft Hydraulic Systems 101

2A6X6 Aircraft Electrical and Environmental Systems 103

2A7X1 Aircraft Metals Technology 105

2A7X2 Nondestructive Inspection 107

2A7X3 Aircraft Structural Maintenance 109

2A7X5 Low Observable Aircraft Structural Maintenance 111

2A8X1 Mobility Air Forces Integrated Communication / Navigation / Mission Systems 113

2A8X2 Mobility Air Forces Integrated Instrument and Flight Control Systems 115

2A9X1 Bomber / Special Integrated Communication / Navigation / Mission Systems 117

2A9X2 Bomber / Special Integrated Instrument and Flight Control Systems 119

2A9X3 Bomber / Special Electronic Warfare and Radar Surveillance Integrated Avionics 121

Fuels Careers(2F) 123

2F0X1 Fuels 125

Logistics Plans Careers(2G) 127

2G0X1 Logistics Plans 129

Missile & Space Systems Maintenance Careers (2M) 131

2M0X1 Missile and Space Systems Electronic Maintenance 133

2M0X2 – Missile and Space Systems Maintenance 135

2M0X3 Missile and Space Facilities 137

Precision Measurement Equipment Laboratory Careers (2P) 139

2P0X1 Precision Measurement Equipment Laboratory 141

Maintenance Management Careers (2R) 143

    2R0X1 Maintenance Management Analysis 145

    2R1X1 Maintenance Management Production 147

Materiel Management Careers (2S) 149

    2S0X1 Materiel Management 151

Transportation & Vehicle Management Careers (2T) 153

    2T0X1 Traffic Management 155

    2T1X1 Ground Transportation 157

    2T2X1 Air Transportation 159

    2T3X1 Mission Generation Vehicular Equipment Maintenance 161

    2T3X7 Fleet Management and Analysis 163

Munitions & Weapons Careers (2W) 165

    2W0X1 Munitions Systems 167

    2W1X1 Aircraft Armament Systems 169

    2W2X1 Nuclear Weapons 171

Cyberspace Support Careers (3D) 173

    3D0X1 Knowledge Operations Management 175

    3D0X2 Cyber Systems Operations 177

    3D0X3 Cyber Surety 179

    3D0X4 Computer Systems Programming 181

    3D1X1 Client Systems 183

    3D1X2 Cyber Transport Systems 185

    3D1X3 Radio Frequency (RF) Transmission Systems 187

    3D1X7 Cable and Antenna Systems 189

Civil Engineering Careers (3E) 191

- 3E0X1 Electrical Systems 193
- 3E0X2 Electrical Power Production 195
- 3E1X1 Heating, Ventilation, Air Conditioning, and Refrigeration 197
- 3E2X1 Pavements and Construction Equipment 199
- 3E3X1 Structural 201
- 3E4X1 Water and Fuel Systems Maintenance 203
- 3E4X3 Pest Management 205
- 3E5X1 Engineering 207
- 3E6X1 Operations Management 209
- 3E7X1 Fire Protection 211
- 3E8X1 Explosive Ordnance Disposal (EOD) 213
- 3E9X1 Emergency Management 215

Force Support Careers (3F) 217
- 3F0X1 Personnel 219
- 3F1X1 Services 221
- 3F5X1 Administration 223

Public Affairs Careers (3N) 225
- 3N0X2 Broadcast Journalist 227
- 3N0X5 Photojournalist 229
- 3N1X1 Regional Band 231
- 3N2X1 Premier Band 233

Security Forces Careers (3P) 235
- 3P0X1 Security Forces 237

Medical Careers (4 Except 4Y) 241
- 4A0X1 Health Services Management 243
- 4A1X1 Medical Materiel 245

- 4A2X1 Biomedical Equipment ... 247
- 4B0X1 Bioenvironmental Engineering (BE) ... 249
- 4C0X1 Mental Health Service ... 251
- 4D0X1 Diet Therapy ... 253
- 4E0X1 Public Health ... 255
- 4H0X1 Cardiopulmonary Laboratory ... 257
- 4J0X2 Physical Medicine ... 259
- 4M0X1 Aerospace and Operational Physiology ... 261
- 4N0X1 Aerospace Medical Service ... 263
- 4N1X1 Surgical Service ... 265
- 4P0X1 Pharmacy Technician ... 267
- 4R0X1 Diagnostic Imaging ... 269
- 4T0X1 Medical Laboratory ... 271
- 4T0X2 Histopathology ... 273
- 4V0X1 Ophthalmic ... 275

Dental Careers (4Y) ... 277
- 4Y0X1 Dental Assistant ... 279
- 4Y0X2 Dental Laboratory ... 281

Paralegal Careers (5J) ... 283
- 5J0X1 Paralegal ... 285

Contracting Careers (6C) ... 287
- 6C0X1 Contracting ... 289

Financial Careers (6F) ... 291
- 6F0X1 Financial Management and Comptroller ... 293

Appendix One: Mechanical AFSCs ... 295

Appendix Two: Administrative AFSCs ... 297

Appendix Three: General AFSCs 299

Appendix Four: Electrical AFSCs 301

Appendix Five: Additional Retraining AFSCs 303

Appendix Six: Special Duty Identifiers (SDI) 305

Appendix Seven: AFSCs Open to Non-US Citizens 307

Appendix Eight: Air Force Eligibility Standards 309

    Personal Beliefs 309

    Religious Accommodation 309

    Drug Use 310

    Height and Weight Requirements 311

    Medical Standards 311

    Age 312

    Citizenship Standards 312

    Dependency Requirements 313

    Education Requirements 314

    Body Alteration/Modification 315

    Prior Service Applicants 315

    Tattoos, Brands, Body Markings 317

    Morals & Legal Issues 317

Air Crew Operations Careers (1A)

Air Crew Operations career fields encompass the pre-flight, in-flight, and post-flight duties of inspecting, training, directing, and performing combat, mobility, and special operations pertinent to enlisted primary aircrew activities.

FUELING OUR LONGER MISSIONS

1A0X1
In-Flight Refueling

Tactical locations are often long distances from supporting airfields, which means aircraft may require refueling midflight. Operating a specialized boom from the back of a KC-135, In-flight Refueling specialists pump thousands of gallons of jet fuel into aircraft in need of fuel. These highly trained experts must have a steady hand and nerves in order to complete this remarkable and crucial task so we can continue to successfully complete all of our missions.

In-flight refueling specialists perform in-flight refueling aircrew duties and Supervise cargo- and passenger-loading and off-loading operations. They ensure availability of fleet service equipment and perform jumpmaster duties when necessary.

Requirements for this Career Field

Qualification for aviation service • Physical qualification for in-flight refueling operation duty • Normal depth perception • Must maintain eligibility to deploy and mobilize worldwide • Height must not be less than 64 inches or more than 77 inches • Completion of a current Single Scope Background Investigation

Relevant Interests & Skills

Aircraft & Flight • Engineering & Applied Science

Training Location

Lackland AFB, TX for 23 days.

Related Civilian Careers
Air Crew Members • Fuel Handling • Cargo Handling

Minimum ASVAB
55 in General

Security Clearance:
Top Secret

Shred-outs:
None

1A2X1
Aircraft Loadmaster

Extensive coordination goes into planning any Air Force flight, especially when transporting both people and supplies. Responsible for properly loading, securing and escorting cargo and passengers, Aircraft Loadmasters custom load aircraft before any flight. From calculating proper weight distribution to providing for passenger comfort throughout the flight, these specialists ensure everything and everyone is safe and secure on flights all over the world.

Aircraft Loadmasters conduct preflight inspection of aircraft and aerospace ground equipment, and supervise the loading and unloading of cargo, vehicles and people on the airplane. They ensure availability of fleet service equipment and passenger comfort items, and conduct in-flight checks on cargo to ensure safety. They also perform scanning duties to detect problems with the airplane or cargo during ground and flying operations.

Requirements for this Career Field
Physical qualification for aircrew duty • Normal depth perception • Qualification for aviation service • Must maintain eligibility to deploy and mobilize worldwide • Height must not be less than 64 inches or more than 77 inches • Completion of a current National Agency Check, Local Agency Checks and Credit (NACLC)

Relevant Interests & Skills
Aircraft & Flight • Logistics & Transportation

Training Location
Lackland AFB, TX for 29 days.

Related Civilian Careers
Cargo Handling Specialists • Production & Operating Worker

Minimum ASVAB
57 in General

Security Clearance
Secret

Shred-outs
None

1A3X1
Airborne Mission Systems Operator

Effective command and control is critical to a mission's success. Responsible for operating the radar, communications and electronic equipment, Airborne Mission Systems Operators help manage the battle space during tactical and strategic missions. Coordinating all of the necessary data received on airborne command centers, these specialists provide critical information to pilots and ground units during missions and operations all over the world.

Aircraft Loadmasters perform aircrew duties on numerous airborne platforms, and inspect and operate airborne communications with ground, air and sea surface units. They perform and supervise airborne equipment operations and maintenance, and determine optimum airborne equipment settings. They also gather, record, and distribute information between our different command units, and they also operate aircraft emergency systems and equipment.

Requirements for this Career Field

Qualification for aviation service • Normal depth perception • Physical qualification for aircrew duty • Must maintain eligibility to deploy and mobilize worldwide • Height not less than 64 inches or more than 77 inches • Physical qualification for voice communications operations • A favorably adjudicated Single Scope Background Investigation is mandatory • Must have a current National Agency check with Law and Credit

Relevant Interests & Skills
Aircraft & Flight • Computers & Computer Science

Training Location
Lackland AFB, TX for 33 days.

Related Civilian Careers
Aircrew Member • Communications Equipment Operator • Electrical Systems Technician

Minimum ASVAB
70 in Electrical

Security Clearance
Secret

Shred-outs
None

1A8X1
Airborne Cryptologic Language Analyst

When we receive or intercept data in the air, it's critical for us to understand it in order to act accordingly. Responsible for translating intelligence communications, Airborne Cryptologic Language Analysts utilize fluent foreign language skills to analyze messages obtained during flight. Providing threat warnings and actionable intelligence that can assist in mission planning, these highly skilled specialists are critical to keeping our missions successful and our Airmen safe.

Airborne Cryptologic Language Analysts intercept and analyze signal intelligence of possible enemy threats, and coordinate with aerospace rescue and recovery services and operations. They improve analytical methods to maximize operational effectiveness, and perform and assist in mission planning. They also provide actionable intelligence to command, and they maintain proficiency in emergency equipment use and procedures.

Requirements for this Career Field
No record or history of temporomandibular joint disorder or pain • A minimum score of 110 on the Defense Language Aptitude Battery; or demonstrated proficiency in a DoD-trained acquisition language with an L2/R2 or better on the Defense Language Proficiency Test (DLPT) or Oral Proficiency Interview (OPI) • Physical qualification for aircrew duty • Qualification for aviation service • Must maintain eligibility to deploy and mobilize worldwide • Height must not be less than 64 inches or

more than 77 inches • Ability to type at a rate of 25 words per minute • When required for a current or pending assignment, must successfully complete a polygraph examination • Completion and favorable adjudication of a current Single Scope Background Investigation

Relevant Interests & Skills
Aircraft & Flight • Computers & Computer Science

Training Location
Lackland AFB, TX; Monterey, CA; and Goodfellow AFB, TX for 224 - 459 days, depending on shred-out assignment.

Related Civilian Careers
Interpreter & Translator • Signals Intelligence Specialist • Intelligence Analysis • Classified Information & Materials Security • Reporter & Correspondent

Minimum ASVAB
72 in General

Security Clearance
Top Secret

Shred-outs
(F) Arabic
(G) Chinese
(H) Korean
(I) Russian
(J) Spanish
(K) Persian
(L) Hebrew
(M) Pashto
(Z) Low-Flow

1A8X2
Airborne Intelligence, Surveillance and Reconnaissance (ISR) Operator

Planning and carrying out missions is dependent upon having the right information at the right time. Responsible for collecting information related to the enemy's strength, movements and activity, Airborne Intelligence, Surveillance and Reconnaissance (ISR) Operators provide top-secret intelligence to command. Utilizing a variety of classified techniques and equipment, these highly trained specialists help ensure we stay ahead of our enemies for the best chance of a mission's success.

Airborne ISR Operators process intelligence information in an airborne environment, and operate, evaluate and manage airborne ISR information and related ground-processing systems. They perform identification, acquisition, analysis and reporting of ISR tasks, and discover, retain, and use knowledge of U.S. and allied operations. They provide threat-warning findings to ground commanders, and they participate in tactical mission planning. They also demonstrate and maintain proficiency in emergency equipment use and procedures.

Requirements for this Career Field
No record or history of temporomandibular joint pain or disorder • Physical qualification for aircrew duty • Qualification for aviation service • Must maintain eligibility to deploy and mobilize worldwide • Height must not be less than 64 inches or more than 77 inches • When required for a current or future

assignment, must successfully complete a polygraph test • Completion of a current Single Scope Background Investigation

Relevant Interests & Skills
Aircraft & Flight • Computers & Computer Science • Intelligence

Training Location
Lackland AFB, TX; and Goodfellow AFB, TX for 66 days.

Related Civilian Careers
Air Crew Member • Intelligence Specialist • Classified Information & Materials Security • Electronic Data Security

Minimum ASVAB
72 in General

Security Clearance
Top Secret

Shred-outs
None

1A9X1
Special Missions Aviation

Many of our aircraft require more than a pilot in order to safely complete each mission. It's the responsibility of Special Missions Aviation specialists to cover everything from pre-flight inspection of aircraft systems to the placement and delivery of all cargo on board. These highly trained specialists have multiple integral roles and monitor all functions for the aircraft, even providing weapon defense when necessary, in order for the team to successfully complete its missions.

Special Missions Aviation specialists complete pre-flight inspection of the aircraft and related aircraft equipment, and assist and coordinate with other positions to ensure sage employment of weapons and defensive systems. They perform in-flight maintenance of airborne weapon systems and associated equipment, and they determine passenger, cargo, fuel and emergency and special equipment distribution and weight. They operate and monitor engine and aircraft system controls and indicators. They also plan, organize, and direct Special Missions Aviation activities.

Requirements for this Career Field

Physical qualification for aircrew duty • Normal depth perception • Qualification for aviation service • Must maintain eligibility to deploy and mobilize worldwide • Height must not be less than 64 inches or more than 77 inches • Must have a current National Agency Check, Local Agency Checks and Credit

Relevant Interests & Skills
Aircraft & Flight • Maintenance & Repair • Weaponry & Materiel

Training Location
Lackland AFB, TX for 27 days.

Related Civilian Careers
Air Crew Member

Minimum ASVAB
60 in Mechanical *and* 57 in General

Security Clearance
Secret

Shred-outs
None

Command and Control Systems Operations Careers (1C)

The Command and Control Systems Operations career fields encompass the functions involved in aerospace surveillance and aerospace vehicle detection, including missile warning systems, controlling, and plotting.

COORDINATING OUR AIRFIELDS

1C0X2
Aviation Resource Management

Completion of missions in the air depends heavily upon our resources on the ground. Responsible for ensuring the coordination of aircraft and crew, Aviation Resource Management specialists make sure that missions run as smoothly as possible. From maintaining flight records to validating aircrew safety requirements, these managers make sure everything and everyone is ready to go and where they need to be so missions can be carried out according to plan.

Aviation Resource Management specialists plan, organize, and direct aircrew and parachutist resource activities. They monitor individual flight requirements, flying hours and aviation requirement changes. They also control security access to Aviation Resource Management Systems data, and they review management procedures and recommend changes.

Requirements for this Career Field
Completion of a current National Agency Check, Local Agency Checks and Credit • Ability to speak distinctly

Relevant Interests & Skills
Aircraft & Flight • Operations & Administration • Logistics & Transportation

Training Location
Keesler AFB, MS for 26 days.

Related Civilian Careers
Airfield Operations Specialist • Licensing Examiner & Inspector • Project/Program Management • Documenting/Record Keeping • Data Entry

Minimum ASVAB
41 in Administrative

Security Clearance
Secret

Shred-outs
None

KEEPING THE AIR SPACE SAFE

1C1X1
Air Traffic Control

The lives of those in the air heavily depend on Airmen on the ground. Responsible for managing the flow of aircraft through all aspects of their flight, Air Traffic Control specialists ensure the safety and efficiency of air traffic on the ground and in the air. Providing specialized skills, these highly trained professionals make quick decisions while monitoring many variables to keep bases, airspace and Airmen all over the world safe.

Air Traffic Control specialists control air traffic by use of visual, radar and non-radar means. They provide a safe and orderly flow of aircraft at the airport and in the air. They also offer emergency assistance to aircraft dealing with a malfunction, and they observe weather conditions and assist aircraft during periods of bad weather.

Requirements for this Career Field

Must earn a minimum score of 55 on the 3-factor model that includes the ASVAB, cognitive, personality (TAPAS) and Air Traffic Scenarios Test (available on Test of Basic Aviation Skills (TBAS) systems). Scores will be calculated on the TBAS system and available on PCSM website for recruiters to review. • Must maintain Ground Based Aircraft Controller Medical Standards • For performance of ATC duties, possession of a Federal Aviation Administration ATC Specialist Certificate • Ability to speak English clearly and distinctly • Completion of a current National Agency Check, Local Agency Checks and Credit

Relevant Interests & Skills
Aircraft & Flight • Operations & Administration • Logistics & Transportation

Training Location
Keesler AFB, MS for 72 days.

Related Civilian Careers
Air Traffic Controller • Mapping Technician • Radio Operator • Computer Operator • Airfield Operations Specialist

Minimum ASVAB
55 in General

Security Clearance
Secret

Shred-outs
None

1C2X1
Combat Control

It takes an incredible amount of skill, physical fitness and courage to carry out some of the Air Force's most difficult missions. As members of Air Force Special Operations, it's the job of Combat Control (CCT) specialists to provide command and control and direct air traffic from remote and sometimes hostile areas. These highly specialized experts are trained in a wide range of skills, including scuba, parachuting, snowmobiling as well as being FAA-certified air traffic controllers in order to establish control and provide combat support on missions all over the globe.

Combat Control specialists deploy into operating locations through whatever means necessary to participate in any mission and they provide command, control, communications and intelligence for a wide array of military missions. They provide air traffic control to service in remote areas and they report current battlefield information to commanders. They operate GPS equipment for targeting assault zones and they also target and control fires to accomplish mission objectives.

Requirements for this Career Field

Successful completion of the Combat Control Team (CCT) physical ability and stamina test (PAST) • Grade of E-5 or below with less than 10 years Total Active Federal Military • Current commander's written recommendation • Completion of the Combat Control Retraining Assessment Process • Physical qualification for air traffic controller duty, marine diving duty, and parachute duty • Qualification to bear firearms • Completion of a current National Agency Check, Local Agency Checks and Credit • Qualification as a static-line parachutist • Qualification as a military freefall parachutist • Qualification as a combat diver

Relevant Interests & Skills
Aircraft & Flight • Intelligence • Special Operations

Training Location
Lackland AFB, TX; Keesler AFB, MS; Ft. Benning, GA; Fairchild AFB, WA; and Pope AFB, NC for 652 days.

Related Civilian Careers
Air Traffic Controller • Communications Equipment Operator • Advanced First Aid • Classified Information & Material Security • Exercise Programs • Firearm Handling and Maintenance • Surveillance • Command & Control Center Specialist

Minimum ASVAB
55 in Mechanical *and* 55 in General

Security Clearance
Secret

Shred-outs
None

1C3X1
Command and Control Operations

The base command post is the central command point for mission operations. It's the job of Command Post specialists to ensure operations and communications run efficiently and effectively under any circumstance. Tasks vary from base to base depending on the resources needed and utilized. These cool-headed professionals provide essential skills and knowledge to keep the base—and our missions—running smoothly.

Command and Control Operations specialists operate command and control facilities, and they keep Air Force commanders advised on the status of all aircraft. They operate equipment to control the launch of missiles. They monitor voice, data and alerting systems. They also compile and maintain entry authority list, directives and daily events log.

Requirements for this Career Field
Ability to speak English clearly and distinctly • Certification by a Command Post Superintendent that the applicant is recommended • No record of mental/emotional instability • Completion of a current Single Scope Background Investigation

Relevant Interests & Skills
Emergency Management & Response • Intelligence • Operations & Administration

Training Location
Keesler AFB, MS for 31 days.

Related Civilian Careers
Command and Control Center Specialist • Emergency Management Specialist • Classified Information & Materials Security • Documenting/Record Keeping • Logistics • Project/Program Management

Minimum ASVAB
55 in Administrative *and* 67 in General

Security Clearance
Top Secret

Shred-outs
None

BRINGING FIREPOWER TO BATTLE

1C4X1
Tactical Air Control Party Specialist

There are few things that can change the course of battle like a properly executed air strike. As members of Air Force Special Operations, Tactical Air Control Party (TACP) specialists imbed with Army and Marine units on the frontline with the incredible responsibility of calling in an air strike on the right target at just the right time. These highly trained experts go through intense physical, mental and technical training in order to withstand the demanding conditions of battle and provide their team with the firepower they need for continued success on the battlefield.

TACP specialists engage enemy forces utilizing advanced technologies and weapon systems, and control and execute operational air and space power. They train in all major climatic conditions: arctic, desert, tropical, ocean and temperate. They operate and maintain cutting-edge technology, including communications, computers, digital networks, targeting and surveillance equipment and various special-purpose tactical vehicles. They target and control surface-to-surface and air-to-surface fires and plan and execute fire missions to accomplish mission objectives. They also engage enemy forces with individual weapons and are trained to administer combat lifesaving assistance.

Requirements for this Career Field

Successful completion of the TACP physical ability and stamina test (PAST) • Minimum score of 30 required on TACP selection model • Normal color vision and depth perception • Compliance with medical standards for Ground Based Controller Duty, including parachute training (as required) and subsequent duty • Must possess a valid state driver's license • Must maintain eligibility to deploy and mobilize worldwide • Qualification to bear firearms • Physical qualification and maintenance of personal physical standards • Completion of a current National Agency Check, Local Agency Checks and Credit

Relevant Interests & Skills
Special Operations • Intelligence • Operations & Administration

Training Location
Lackland AFB, TX; Fairchild AFB, WA; and Ft. Benning, GA for 390 days.

Related Civilian Careers
Command and Control Center Specialist • Artillery and Missile Crew • Advance First Aid • Classified Information & Materials Security • Emergency Medical Care • Exercise Programs • Firearm Handling & Maintenance • Intelligence Analyst • Protective Services • Surveillance

Minimum ASVAB
49 in General

Security Clearance
Secret

Shred-outs
None

1C5X1
Command and Control Battle Management Operations

Ensuring our nation's security requires constant vigilance. Responsible for providing radar control and monitoring of global airspace, Command and Control Battle Management Operations specialists keep a watchful eye on everything that goes on in the sky. These highly trained experts operate sophisticated radar and electronic systems from locations all over the world, fulfilling a role crucial to the success of our missions and vital to safeguarding our nation.

Command and Control Battle Management Operations specialists manage and operate Command and Control Battle Management Operations systems. They conduct mission planning, and interpret and react to radar data and console displays. They gather, record and distribute operational information among air defense and air traffic control agencies. They also test and evaluate the capabilities of new equipment.

Requirements for this Career Field

Normal color vision • Member must be qualified for Ground Based Controller duties • Must possess a valid state/territory driver's license • Ability to speak English clearly and distinctly • Must maintain eligibility to deploy and mobilize worldwide • Completion of a current National Agency Check, Local Agency Checks and Credit

Relevant Interests & Skills
Electronics & Electrical • Operations & Administration

Training Location
Keesler AFB, MS for 30 days.

Related Civilian Careers
Command and Control Center Specialist • Communication Equipment Operator • Cargo Handling Specialist • Electronic & Electrical Repairer • Electrical Engineering Technician • Surveillance

Minimum ASVAB
55 in General

Security Clearance
Secret

Shred-outs
(D) Weapons Director

1C6X1
Space Systems Operations

Operating the largest space program in the world takes the combined efforts and skills of thousands of Airmen. It's the responsibility of Space Systems Operations specialist to do everything from detecting sea-launched ballistic missiles and tracking satellites to assisting in rocket launches and space flight operations. These highly trained experts must be able to stay calm under pressure and utilize an incredible amount of skill to effectively perform the multiple tasks vital to Air Force missions.

Space Systems Operations specialists detect, identify and maintain orbital parameters on earth satellite vehicles. They operate defensive and offensive space control systems, and detect and track missile launches. They perform launch and on-orbit operations for military satellites, and perform range operations in support of ballistic missile and space launches. They ensure operational effectiveness and suitability of space capabilities through operational testing and evaluation.

Requirements for this Career Field
Normal color vision • Submission of a Single Scope Background Investigation

Relevant Interests & Skills
Space • Operations & Administration

Training Location
Vandenburg AFB, CA for 51 - 100 days.

Related Civilian Careers
Radar and Sonar Technician • Space Operations • Electrical Engineering Technician • Electrical & Electronics Repairer

Minimum ASVAB
70 in Electrical

Security Clearance
Top Secret

Shred-outs
None

1C7X1
Airfield Management

The safety of our Airmen depends as much on the upkeep of the airfields it does our planes. Responsible for the maintenance of runways, lighting and other airfield components and systems, Airfield Management specialists ensure that all takeoffs and landings can proceed without incident. From keeping runways clear of foreign objects to communicating hazards to pilots, these professionals make sure our aircraft maintain their ability to take off at a moment's notice.

Airfield Management specialists manage airfield operations to ensure a safe, efficient and effective airfield environment. They provide aircrews with preflight briefings, and inspect runways, taxiways, parking aprons, lighting and airfield clearance areas. They utilize air-to-ground and land-mobile radios to coordinate airfield operations with aircraft. They also respond to flight safety hazards affecting the airfield environment.

Requirements for this Career Field
Normal color vision • Ability to speak distinctly in person and over air-to-ground radios • Must possess a valid state driver's license • Completion of a current National Agency Check, Local Agency Checks and Credit

Relevant Interests & Skills
Logistics & Transportation • Operations & Administration

Training Location
Keesler AFB, MS for 30 days.

Related Civilian Careers
Airfield Operations Specialist • Flight Operations Specialist • Documenting/Record Keeping • Power Distributor & Dispatcher

Minimum ASVAB
40 in Mechanical *and* 50 in General

Security Clearance
Secret

Shred-outs
None

KEEPING AIRCRAFT IN CONTACT

1C8X3
Radar, Airfield, & Weather Systems (RAWS)

Keeping in constant contact with our planes is essential to managing missions and airspace. Responsible for installing and maintaining radio, navigation and meteorological systems, Airfield Systems specialists make sure we're always able to track and communicate with our aircraft. From installing ground-to-air radio systems to ensuring proper system operation, these professionals play an integral role in keeping our aircraft safe and helping our Airmen accomplish their mission.

Airfield Systems specialists install, remove, and maintain navigation and air traffic control ground-to-air radio systems. They supervise meteorological and navigation systems maintenance activities, and resolve technical problems and improve maintenance techniques. They prepare equipment for deployment, and supervise Airfield Systems maintenance activities.

Requirements for this Career Field
Normal color vision • Must possess a valid state driver's license • Freedom from fear of heights • Completion of a current National Agency Check, Local Agency Checks and Credit

Relevant Interests & Skills
Operations & Administration

Training Location
Keesler AFB, MS for 139 days.

Related Civilian Careers
Electrical and Electronics Repairer • Telecommunications Technician • Robotics Technician • Industrial Machinery Mechanic • Signal & Track Switch Repairer

Minimum ASVAB
70 in Electrical

Security Clearance
Secret

Shred-outs
None

Intelligence Careers (1N)

The Intelligence career fields encompass functions involved in collecting, producing, and distributing data that have strategic, tactical, or technical value from an intelligence viewpoint.

1N0X1
Operations Intelligence

The success of any mission depends just as much on the planning and intelligence behind it as the Airmen who are carrying it out. Working as part of a team, Operations Intelligence specialists analyze raw data, looking for usable intelligence. Fulfilling a critical role, these experts receive, analyze, report and disseminate information for key elements to help ensure our Airmen have the intelligence they need to remain safe and successfully complete their missions.

Operations Intelligence specialists provide analysis of adversary threat systems and intelligence expertise necessary for mission plans. They conduct external intelligence training on collecting and reporting requirements and procedures, and they prepare and present intelligence reports and briefings to commanders and aircrews. They assess vulnerability of U.S. forces' telecommunications networks and information which could be collected and exploited by adversaries.

Requirements for this Career Field
No speech disorders or noticeable communications deficiencies • When required for a current or future assignment, must successfully complete a polygraph test • Completion of a current Single Scope Background Investigation

Relevant Interests & Skills
Operations & Administration • Computers & Computer Science • Intelligence

Training Location
Goodfellow AFB, TX for 110 days.

Related Civilian Careers
Command and Control Center Specialist • Classified Information & Materials Security • Electronic Data Security Specialist • Intelligence Analyst • Surveillance

Minimum ASVAB
64 in Administrative

Security Clearance
Top Secret

Shred-outs
None

1N1X1
Geospatial Intelligence

Some of our most critical intelligence comes from keen eyes spotting miniscule details in aerial imagery. Responsible for analyzing imagery from satellites, remotely piloted vehicles and other sources, Geospatial Intelligence specialists discern what is normal and what could be a threat. These highly trained experts perform a wide array of intelligence activities that include exploitation, development and distribution of multi-sensor geospatial intelligence products to support the needs of any of our missions.

Geospatial Intelligence specialists exploit and analyze multi-sensor imagery and geospatial data. They analyze terrain and structures to determine usability and possible threats, and they utilize maps to determine location and distance from target. They prepare and present intelligence reports and compile and maintain imagery and target folders.

Requirements for this Career Field

Normal color vision • Stereopsis (depth perception) acuity equivalent to depth perception standards for flying Class I or Class IA with or without correction • When required for a current or future assignment, must successfully complete a polygraph test • Require completion of a current Single Scope Background Investigation

Relevant Interests & Skills
Future Technologies • Computers & Computer Science • Intelligence

Training Location
Goodfellow AFB, TX for 100 - 112 days.

Related Civilian Careers
Cartographer and Photogrammetrist • Classified Information & Materials Security • Intelligence • Surveillance • Message Traffic Analysis • Mapping Technician

Minimum ASVAB
66 in General

Security Clearance
Top Secret

Shred-outs
(A) Imagery Analyst
(B) Targeteer

GATHERING INFO FROM THE AIR

1N2X1
Signals Intelligence Analyst

As technology becomes more sophisticated, so does the way we have to gather and interpret information. Utilizing sophisticated equipment, Signals Intelligence Analysts extract, analyze and identify foreign activity and communication that come from electromagnetic emissions. These analysts relay their findings by producing combat, strategic and tactical intelligence reports and notify the appropriate commanders of unusual activity or critical situations so we can respond with the necessary speed, force and precision.

Signals Intelligence Analyst specialists operate electronic equipment and computer systems to exploit signal intelligence. They manipulate and extract intelligence data from electromagnetic emissions, and they use classified reference materials to develop your ability to interpret and analyze signals. They also update national databases with findings.

Requirements for this Career Field
When required for a current or future assignment, must successfully complete and pass a Counter Intelligence polygraph test • Completion of a current Single Scope Background Investigation

Relevant Interests & Skills
Computers & Computer Science • Intelligence

Training Location
Goodfellow AFB, TX for 74 - 84 days.

Related Civilian Careers
Command and Control Center Specialist • Classified Information & Materials Security • Data Entry • Documenting/Record Keeping • Electronic Data Security • Intelligence • Surveillance

Minimum ASVAB
72 in General for 1N2X1A • 72 in General *or* 67 in General *and* 60 on Cyber-Test for 1N2X1C

Security Clearance
Top Secret

Shred-outs
(A) Electronic
(C) Communications

DECIPHERING EVERY MESSAGE

1N3X1
Cryptologic Language Analyst

Intelligence around the world comes in many forms, and often it's in a foreign language. Responsible for translating and analyzing messages, Cryptologic Language Analysts provide vital intelligence to decision-makers. Proficient in a language like Arabic, Chinese, Korean, Russian, Spanish, Persian Farsi, Hebrew, Pashto or Urdu, these skilled specialists play an essential role in helping us complete our mission and keep our country safe.

Cryptologic Language Analyst specialists use foreign language skills to search for, identify and process other communications. They operate voice and graphic communications equipment. They transcribe, translate and summarize intercepted voice and graphic communications, and they provide warning of adversarial intentions against the U.S. They also identify regional and cultural factors associated with activities of interest.

Requirements for this Career Field

No record or history of temporomandibular joint disorder or pain • A minimum score of 110 on the Defense Language Aptitude Battery; or demonstrated proficiency in a DoD-trained acquisition language with an L2/R2 or better on the (DLPT) or OPI equivalent • Ability to type at a rate of 25 words per minute • When required for a current or pending assignment, must successfully complete a polygraph examination • Completion and favorable adjudication of a current Single Scope Background Investigation

Relevant Interests & Skills
Arts & Humanity • Intelligence

Training Location
Monterey, CA; and Goodfellow AFB, TX for 240 - 480 days.

Related Civilian Careers
Interpreter & Translator • Intelligence • Classified Information & Materials Security • Foreign Language Specialist • Editor • Reporter & Correspondent

Minimum ASVAB
72 in General

Security Clearance
Top Secret

Shred-outs
(F) Arabic
(G) Chinese
(H) Korean
(I) Russian
(J) Spanish
(K) Persian
(L) Hebrew
(M) Pashto
(N) Urdu
(Z) Low-Flow

1N4X1
Fusion Analyst

Intelligence is one of the best and most important weapons at our disposal. Responsible for acquiring and analyzing information, Fusion Analysts determine the value and implications of intelligence we receive from target network communications. Through research and assessment, these specialists gauge the impact of the information and distribute their findings to high-level decision-makers so we can take timely action to ensure the safety of Airmen and our country.

Fusion Analyst specialists identify and interpret real-time threat warning data, and advise commanders on force protection and intelligence information. They exploit global communications to support Computer Network Operations, and they isolate essential elements of information. They also analyze and report intelligence information, and they gain and maintain knowledge of global communications procedures.

Requirements for this Career Field

No speech disorders or noticeable communications deficiencies • Minimum score of 46 required on the Tailored Adaptive Personality Assessment System • Successfully complete and pass a Counter Intelligence (CI) polygraph test • Completion of the Joint Cyber Analysis course is mandatory for those in grades E-6 and below with less than 15 Years of time in service • Completion and favorable adjudication of a current Single Scope Background Investigation

Relevant Interests & Skills
Engineering & Applied Science • Natural Science

Training Location
Goodfellow AFB, TX for 110 days.

Related Civilian Careers
Command & Control Center Specialist • Data Analyst • Intelligence • Classified Information & Materials Security • Data Entry • Documenting/Record Keeping • Electronic Data Security • Surveillance

Minimum ASVAB
62 in General, *or* 57 in General *and* 60 on Cyber-Test for 1N4X1A • 62 in General for 1N4X1B

Security Clearance
Top Secret

Shred-outs
(A) Digital Network Analyst
(B) Analysis and Production

Aircrew Flight Equipment Careers (1P)

The Aircrew Flight Equipment field encompasses functions that enhance aircrew performance through the proper equipment integration of the human and the aircraft.

1P0X1
Aircrew Flight Equipment

Part of preparing a plane for flight is making sure they're equipped with supplies for any situation. Responsible for ensuring that all flight and safety equipment is in perfect working order, Aircrew Flight Equipment specialists make sure Airmen have the supplies necessary for any situation. From packing emergency items like parachutes and survival kits to maintaining regularly used items like flight helmets and oxygen masks, the attention to detail provided by these professionals could mean the difference between life and death.

Aircrew Flight Equipment specialists manage the inspection, maintenance and adjustments to assigned aircrew flight equipment. They operate various types of test equipment such as oxygen and leakage testers, and they control and issue aircrew side arms and ammunition. They perform operator maintenance and service inspections on shop equipment. They instruct aircrews on the purpose and use of their flight and chemical defense equipment, and they also ensure aircrew are weapons-qualified and prepared to deploy.

Requirements for this Career Field
Must possess a valid state driver's license • Normal color vision • Ability to speak clearly and distinctly • Visual acuity correctable to 20/20 • No record of claustrophobia or claustrophobic tendencies • Completion of a current National Agency Check, Local Agency Checks and Credit • Qualification to bear firearms

Relevant Interests & Skills
Future Technologies • Natural Science

Training Location
Sheppard AFB, TX for 56 days.

Related Civilian Careers
Installation, Maintenance and Repair Worker • Survival Equipment Technician • Classified Information & Materials Security • Electrical Engineer Technician • Fabric Working/Tailoring • Fire & Hazardous Material • Firearm Handling & Maintenance

Minimum ASVAB
40 in Mechanical

Security Clearance
Secret

Shred-outs
None

Aircrew Protection Careers (1T)

The Aircrew Protection career field encompasses the functions involved in instructing aircrew and other designated personnel on the principles, procedures, and techniques of global survival; and locating and penetrating incident areas to provide emergency medical treatment, survival, and evacuation of survivors.

1T0X1
Survival, Evasion, Resistance and Escape (SERE)

Every member of an aircrew must be able to survive on their own in any environment under any condition should their aircraft go down. Survival, Evasion, Resistance and Escape (SERE) specialists teach Airmen everything they need to know to do just that. From building shelters and procuring water to land navigation and evasion techniques, these highly trained experts impart the skills needed for Airmen to survive on their own and evade the enemy until they can be rescued and brought home.

SERE specialists conduct operations around the world preparing aircrew and high-risk-of-isolation personnel to return from any type of survival situation. They train in all major climatic conditions: arctic, desert, tropical, ocean and temperate. They organize and conduct SERE training activities and instruct on the use of related equipment. They perform parachuting duties and also determine readiness of equipment and Airmen.

Requirements for this Career Field

Completion of high school with eleventh-grade reading level • Successful completion of the SERE physical ability and stamina test • Prior to attendance of SERE Training, applicants must meet physical and psychological qualifications • Absence of any speech impediment • Ability to read aloud and speak distinctly • Normal color vision • Completion of a current National Agency Check, Local Agency Checks and Credit

Relevant Interests & Skills
Special Operations • Natural Science

Training Location
Lackland AFB, TX for 15 days.

Related Civilian Careers
Teacher and Instructor • Military/Tactical Training • Emergency Medical Care • Classified Information & Materials • Exercise Programs • Firearm Handling & Maintenance • Intelligence • Protective Services • Surveillance

Minimum ASVAB
55 in General

Security Clearance
Secret

Shred-outs
None

1T2X1
Pararescue

When an Airman needs saving, it's our duty to do everything we can to bring them home. As members of Air Force Special Operations, Pararescue (PJ) specialists rescue and recover downed aircrews from hostile or otherwise unreachable areas. These highly trained experts perform rescues in every type of terrain and partake in every part of the mission, from search and rescue, to combat support to providing emergency medical treatment, in order to ensure that every mission is a successful one.

Pararescue specialists use survival techniques to help provide for the survival of others. They perform, lead and supervise pararescue activities. They study terrain and situation surrounding the mission, and perform aerial and surface deployment methods to reach objective area. They conduct discrete surface-to-air signaling, and utilize firearms to provide security on the mission. They also provide emergency trauma and medical care.

Requirements for this Career Field

Successful completion of the Pararescue physical ability and stamina test • Grade of E-5 or below with less than 10 years Total Active Federal Military Service • Current commander's written recommendation • Completion of the Pararescue Retraining Assessment • Physical qualification for aircrew, parachute, and marine diving duty • Qualification, currency, and proficiency as a static line and military freefall parachutist, and as a military scuba diver • Certification from the National Registry (or State) for

Emergency Medical Technicians as an emergency medical technician • Physical certification and maintenance of personal physical standards • Completion of a current National Agency Check, Local Agency Checks and Credit

Relevant Interests & Skills
Intelligence • Emergency Management & Response • Special Operations • Health & Medicine • Health Technicians & Specialists

Training Location
Lackland AFB, TX for 501 days.

Related Civilian Careers
Search and Rescue • Special Forces • Advanced First Aid • Classified Information & Materials Security • Electrical Repairer • Exercise Programs • Firearm Handling & Maintenance • Surveillance

Minimum ASVAB
44 in General

Security Clearance
Secret

Shred-outs
None

Remotely Piloted Aircraft Sensor Operator Careers (1U)

The Remotely Piloted Aircraft (RPA) Sensor Operator career field encompasses functions involved in program formulating, policy planning, inspecting, training, and performing combat and operations related to crew position activities, sensor suite operations and unit functionality.

1U0X1
Remotely Piloted Aircraft (RPA) Sensor Operator

As our country's preeminent air defense, a lot of what we do, from surveillance to weapons, happens in the skies. Providing our forces with the intelligence they need, Remotely Piloted Aircraft (RPA) Sensor Operators play an integral role in helping forces know what actions to take. Utilizing state-of-the-art equipment, these highly trained experts perform surveillance and reconnaissance and provide close air support and real-time battle damage assessment, playing a vital role in ensuring our missions succeed.

RPA Sensor Operator specialists perform intelligence surveillance and reconnaissance. They detect, analyze and discriminate between valid and invalid targets. They assist in air navigation, fire control planning and determining effective weapons control and delivery tactics. They conduct immediate first phase Battle Damage Assessments. They perform pre- and in-flight mission planning activities, and test and evaluate capabilities of new equipment and propriety of new procedures.

Requirements for this Career Field
Normal color vision • Ground Based Aircraft Controller Physical • Qualification for aviation service • Completion of a current Single Scope Background Investigation

Relevant Interests & Skills

Intelligence • Computers & Computer Science • Weaponry & Materiel • Aircraft & Flight • Electronics & Electrical • Future Technologies

Training Location

Lackland AFB, TX; and Randolph AFB, TX for 31 days.

Related Civilian Careers

Electro-Mechanical Technician • Aircraft Design • Electrical Engineering Technician • Intelligence • Piloting & Navigating • Process Analysis • Technical Writing

Minimum ASVAB

64 in General *or* 54 in Electrical

Security Clearance

Top Secret

Shred-outs

None

Weather Careers (1W)

The Weather career field encompasses collecting, analyzing, predicting, tailoring, and integrating weather and space environmental information, including forecasts of conditions, to provide decision-quality information on environmental impacts to Air Force, Army, Joint and Coalition operations.

1W0X1 Weather

Countless factors can contribute to the outcome of a mission, including something as seemingly simple as the weather. It's the job of Weather specialists to keep a constant watch over the forecast and conditions that can affect the safety of pilots and aircrew. These experts utilize the latest technology to predict weather patterns, prepare forecasts and communicate weather information to commanders and pilots so that every mission goes as planned.

Weather specialists analyze weather conditions, prepare forecasts, issue weather warnings and brief weather information to pilots. They observe, record and transmit space environment observations, and they read and interpret weather satellite imagery, climatology reports, computerized weather prediction models and Doppler weather radar imagery. They also understand war fighter tactics and its relationship to weather conditions.

Requirements for this Career Field
Ability to speak distinctly • Visual acuity correctible to 20/20 • Completion of a current National Agency Check, Local Agency Checks and Credit

Relevant Interests & Skills
Future Technologies • Natural Science • Computers & Computer Science

Training Location
Keesler AFB, MS for 146 days.

Related Civilian Careers
Life, Physical & Social Science Technician • Reporter, Correspondent, and Broadcast Specialist • Atmospheric Analysis & Forecasting • Electronic Equipment • Project/Program Management • Proofreading/Editing • Scientific Research • Technical Writing

Minimum ASVAB
66 in General *and* 50 in Electrical

Security Clearance
Secret

Shred-outs
None

1W0X2
Special Operations Weather Technician

In our joint effort to defend our country, select Airmen imbed with Army or Marine Special Forces units. As members of Air Force Special Operations, Special Operations Weather Technicians (SOWT) provide the information their teams need to successfully complete their missions. Utilizing high-tech atmospheric instruments, these highly specialized experts retrieve data from radar and weather satellites to relay to the teams as they carry out high-risk missions in a variety of conditions all over the world.

SOWT specialists plan, supervise, give instructions and perform evaluations on special operations weather teams. They collect, analyze and predict oceanographic, meteorological and space atmosphere conditions. They prepare reports on weather advisories, warnings and inclement environmental conditions and they collect weather data, observe meteorological conditions and integrate into military-making decisions. They read and interpret weather satellite imagery, climatology reports and computerized weather prediction. They deploy into remote areas and locations to participate in military operations and they utilize demolitions to create or remove obstacles.

Requirements for this Career Field

Ability to speak English distinctly • Successful completion of the Special Operations Weather physical ability and stamina test • Minimum score of 30 required on SOWT selection • Physical qualification and maintenance of physical standards for special operations to include parachute • Must possess a valid state driver's • Qualification to bear firearms • Qualification, currency, and proficiency in military parachute operations • Completion of a current National Agency Check, Local Agency Checks and Credit

Relevant Interests & Skills
Future Technologies • Intelligence • Special Operations • Natural Science

Training Location
Lackland AFB, TX; Keesler AFB, MS; Ft. Benning, GA; Fairchild AFB, WA; and Pope AFB, NC for 967 days.

Related Civilian Careers
Life, Physical & Social Science Technician • Advanced First Aid • Atmospheric Analysis & Forecasting • Electronic Device Repair • Hydrological Analysis & Forecasting • Surveillance

Minimum ASVAB
66 in General *and* 50 in Electrical

Security Clearance
Secret

Shred-outs
None

Aerospace Maintenance Careers (2A)

The Aerospace Maintenance career field encompasses installing, maintaining, calibrating, repairing, modifying, and removing aircraft components from various systems, including but not limited to avionics, communication and navigation systems, radar and warfare systems, aircrew egress, fuel, pneudraulic, engines, propellers, electrical, and environmental systems.

2A0X1
Avionics Test Station and Components

Air Force aircraft are equipped with some of the world's most sophisticated electronic systems. Avionics Test Station and Components specialists are responsible for ensuring that these systems remain perfectly calibrated. These professionals inspect and maintain everything from aircraft radar and weapons control to the testing equipment essential to the maintenance process. So when our aircraft are deployed, every system is in perfect working order.

Avionics Test Station and Components specialists maintain aircraft electronic equipment such as radar and navigation systems. They perform operational tests on test equipment, support equipment and aircraft components. They repair both the aircraft equipment and the associated test equipment. They also organize the facilities to ensure parts are stocked and available.

Requirements for this Career Field
Normal color vision • Completion of a current National Agency Check, Local Agency Checks and Credit

Relevant Interests & Skills
Aircraft & Flight • Electronics & Electrical

Training Location
Sheppard AFB, TX for 73 - 90 days.

Related Civilian Careers
Aircraft Mechanic & Service Technician • Avionics Technician • Electrical & Electronics Repairer • Electrical Engineering Technician • Manufacturing Production Technician • Mechanical Engineering Technician

Minimum ASVAB
70 in Electrical

Security Clearance
Secret

Shred-outs
(K) A-10/B-2/C-17/CV-22/F-16/AFSOC Avionics Systems
(M) B-1/E-8/F-15 Avionics Systems
(P) Avionics Sensor Systems and Electronic Warfare Systems

2A2X1
Special Operations Forces/Personnel Recovery (SOF/PR) Integrated Communication / Navigation / Mission Systems

The systems onboard our aircraft play an integral part on any successful air mission. It's the job of Special Operations Forces/Personnel Recovery Integrated Communications / Navigation / Mission Systems specialists to provide the precision maintenance necessary to keep each of these systems running perfectly. These experts utilize a variety of methods, including schematic and wiring diagrams, to ensure these systems are able to meet the needs of the pilots throughout every mission.

These specialists operate and maintain communication, navigation and missions systems. They remove, install, check and repair avionics systems and line replaceable units and diagnose malfunctions using test systems and equipment. They prepare aircraft for covert operations and reconnaissance and review maintenance data to determine possible trends.

Requirements for this Career Field
Normal color vision • Completion of a current National Agency Check, Local Agency Checks and Credit

Relevant Interests & Skills
Electronics & Electrical

Training Location
Sheppard AFB, TX for 117 days.

Related Civilian Careers
Aircraft Mechanic & Service Technician • Avionics Technician • Electrical & Electronics Repairer • Electrical Engineering Technician • Manufacturing Production Technician • Mechanical Engineering Technician

Minimum ASVAB
70 in Electrical

Security Clearance
Secret

Shred-outs
(A) CV-22

2A2X2
Special Operations Forces/Personnel Recovery (SOF/PR) Integrated Instrument and Flight Control Systems

When it comes to our advanced aircraft, there is no margin for system errors. It is the job of Special Operations Forces/Personnel Recovery Integrated Instrument and Flight Control Systems specialists to ensure that special operations planes are well maintained and remain in perfect working condition. Utilizing a variety of tools and methods, these experts test systems to locate malfunctions and repair them so that the aircraft are able to complete each mission with no concerns.

These specialists operate and maintain instrument and flight control systems. They remove, install, check and repair avionics systems in line replaceable units, and they diagnose malfunctions using test systems and equipment. They prepare aircraft for covert operations and reconnaissance. They also review maintenance data to determine possible trends.

Requirements for this Career Field
Normal color vision • Completion of a current National Agency Check, Local Agency Checks and Credit

Relevant Interests & Skills
Electronics & Electrical • Computers & Computer Science

Training Location
Sheppard AFB, TX; and Keesler AFB, MS for 83 - 119 days.

Related Civilian Careers
Aircraft Mechanic & Service Technician • Avionics Technician • Electrical & Electronics Repairer • Electrical Engineering Technician • Manufacturing Production Technician • Mechanical Engineering Technician

Minimum ASVAB
70 in Electrical

Security Clearance
Secret

Shred-outs
None

2A2X3
Special Operations Forces/Personnel Recovery (SOF/PR) Integrated Electronic Warfare Systems

As technology advances, our aircraft are able to provide greater defensive advantages to the pilots flying them. Responsible for analyzing systems and repairing any found malfunctions, Special Operations Forces/Personnel Recovery Integrated Electronic Warfare Systems specialists ensure that pilots are always able to detect the threats and risks present while on their missions. These experts utilize a variety of systems and methods to make certain that every system is working exactly as it should when it takes to the air.

These specialists operate and maintain electronic warfare systems. They remove, install, check and repair avionics systems in line replaceable units, and they diagnose malfunctions using test systems and equipment. They prepare aircraft for covert operations and reconnaissance, as well as review maintenance data to determine possible trends.

Requirements for this Career Field
Normal color vision • Completion of a current National Agency Check, Local Agency Checks and Credit

Relevant Interests & Skills
Electronics & Electrical • Computers & Computer Science

Training Location
Sheppard AFB, TX for 100 days.

Related Civilian Careers
Aircraft Mechanic & Service Technician • Avionics Technician • Electrical & Electronics Repairer • Electrical Engineering Technician • Manufacturing Production Technician • Mechanical Engineering Technician

Minimum ASVAB
70 in Electrical

Security Clearance
Secret

Shred-outs
(A) CV-22

KEEPING SPECIALIZED AIRCRAFT AIRBORNE

2A3X3
Tactical Aircraft Maintenance

The Air Force employs hundreds of tactical aircraft to complete our missions, including fighters, strike-fighters and attack planes. It's the responsibility of Tactical Aircraft Maintenance specialists to ensure that every component of these high performance aircraft is maintained to the most exacting standards. These experts ensure that the aircraft in their care are ready to fly at a moment's notice so that pilots can safely and effectively complete their mission.

Tactical Aircraft Maintenance specialists perform special pre- and postflight inspections. They use automated technical data to diagnose and solve maintenance problems and they supervise and perform aircraft, engine and component inspections. They conduct functional tests of repaired engines, and supervise and assist in recovering aircrafts. They also review maintenance data to spot potential trends

Requirements for this Career Field
Normal color vision • Completed and current National Agency Check, Local Agency Checks and Credit

Relevant Interests & Skills
Aircraft & Flight • Electronics & Electrical • Maintenance & Repair

Training Location
Sheppard AFB, TX. Length varies with which aircraft being trained for.

Related Civilian Careers
Aircraft Mechanic & Service Technician • Industrial Machinery Mechanic • Mechanical Engineering Technician • Electrical & Electronics Repairer

Minimum ASVAB
47 in Mechanical

Security Clearance
None

Shred-outs
(E) A-10/U-2
(L) F-15
(M) F-16

2A3X4
Fighter Aircraft Integrated Avionics

A pilot's ability to process information and make quick decisions is crucial to completing their mission. Their success hinges on highly sophisticated avionics systems. Responsible for maintaining and repairing these systems, Fighter Aircraft Integrated Avionics specialists ensure that pilots can receive the information they need to successfully operate their aircraft. Keeping a trained eye on everything from communications systems to flight controls, these experts are critical to the advancement and safety of our missions.

Fighter Aircraft Integrated Avionics specialists remove, install and check integrated avionics systems. They trace data flow and wiring diagrams, and they inspect, troubleshoot and maintain aircraft wiring system. They check externally mounted avionics systems, and recommend methods to improve equipment performance.

Requirements for this Career Field
Normal color vision • Completion of a current National Agency Check, Local Agency Checks and Credit

Relevant Interests & Skills
Aircraft & Flight • Electronics & Electrical • Computers & Computer Science • Maintenance & Repair

Training Location
Sheppard AFB, TX for 109 - 126 days.

Related Civilian Careers
Aircraft Mechanic & Service Technician • Avionics Technician • Electrical & Electronics Repairer • Electrical Engineering Technician • Manufacturing Production Technician • Mechanical Engineering Technician

Minimum ASVAB
70 in Electrical

Security Clearance
Secret

Shred-outs
(A) A-10/U-2 Avionics
(B) F-15 Avionics
(C) F-16 Avionics

2A3X5
Advanced Fighter Aircraft Integrated Avionics

This AFSC is the same as 2A3X4 in all aspects, except for the aircraft shred-outs, which are :
(A) F-22
(B) F-35
(C) MQ-1, MQ-9, RQ-4

2A3X7
Tactical Aircraft Maintenance (5th Generation)

This AFSC is the same as 2A3X3 in all aspects, except for the aircraft shred-outs, which are :
(A) F-22
(B) F-35

2A3X8
Remotely Piloted Aircraft Maintenance

It's essential that all of our Aircraft be well maintained, especially when they function with no one on board. It's the job of Remotely Piloted Aircraft Maintenance Specialists to ensure that each RPA works at its optimal performance. These experts utilize state-of-the-art equipment to ensure the aircraft are able to maneuver perfectly through combat environments to pinpoint the targets critical to our missions.

Remotely Piloted Aircraft Maintenance specialists maintain aircraft, support equipment, forms and records. They perform pre-, thru- and postflight inspections. They diagnose and solve maintenance problems on aircraft systems, and they remove and install aircraft engine components. They inspect and identify aircraft corrosion for prevention and repair. They also supervise and assist in launching and recovering aircraft

Requirements for this Career Field
Normal color vision • Completion of a current National Agency Check, Local Agency Checks and Credit

Relevant Interests & Skills
Aircraft & Flight • Electronics & Electrical • Maintenance & Repair

Training Location
Sheppard AFB, TX. Length varies with which aircraft being trained for.

Related Civilian Careers
Aircraft Mechanic & Service Technician • Industrial Machinery Mechanic • Mechanical Engineering Technician • Automotive/Mobile Equipment Maintenance • Electrical & Electronics Repairer

Minimum ASVAB
47 in Mechanical

Security Clearance
Secret

Shred-outs
(A) MQ-1/MQ-9
(B) RQ-4

2A5X1
Airlift / Special Mission Aircraft Maintenance

We do everything we can to keep our aircraft in peak condition at all times. Conducting pre- and postflight inspections, Airlift/Special Mission Aircraft Maintenance specialists ensure that all our aircraft are operational and ready to fly. Primarily responsible for general maintenance, these technicians also determine when repairs require the focus of an individual systems specialist so the aircraft are ready to go whenever they're needed.

Airlift / Special Mission Aircraft Maintenance specialists maintain aircraft, support equipment, forms and records, and they perform aircraft inspections and advise on problems, maintenance and servicing. They interpret and discuss inspection findings, and they supervise and assist in launching and recovering aircraft

Requirements for this Career Field
Normal color vision • Completion of a current National Agency Check, Local Agency Checks and Credit

Relevant Interests & Skills
Aircraft & Flight • Maintenance & Repair

Training Location
Sheppard AFB, TX. Length varies with which aircraft being trained for.

Related Civilian Careers
Aircraft Mechanic & Service Technician • Industrial Machinery Mechanic • Mechanical Engineering Technician • Automotive/Mobile Equipment Maintenance • Electrical & Electronics Repairer Mechanic • Inventory Management Specialist

Minimum ASVAB
47 in Mechanical

Security Clearance
Secret

Shred-outs
(A) C-20/C-21/C-37/C-40/E-4/VC-25
(B) C-130/C-27J
(C) C-5
(D) C-17

2A5X2
Helicopter / Tiltrotor Aircraft Maintenance

Helicopters play a large and indispensable role in Air Force missions. Providing essential service and maintenance, Helicopter/Tiltrotor Aircraft Maintenance specialists keep these incredibly technical aircraft operating at optimal performance levels. More than just ensuring the aircraft are in working order, these highly trained professionals disassemble and reassemble them for transportation to locations where they're most needed all over the world.

Helicopter / Tiltrotor Aircraft Maintenance specialists perform preventive maintenance by inspecting and functionally checking structures and systems. They adjust, align, and calibrate aircraft systems, and use technical data to diagnose and solve maintenance problems. They prepare aircraft for movement to and from various locations. They also coordinate maintenance plans and schedules to meet operational requirements.

Requirements for this Career Field
Normal color vision • Completion of a current National Agency Check, Local Agency Checks and Credit

Relevant Interests & Skills
Aircraft & Flight • Maintenance & Repair

Training Location
Locations vary. Length varies with which aircraft being trained for.

Related Civilian Careers
Aircraft Mechanic & Service Technician • Industrial Machinery Mechanic • Mechanical Engineering Technician • Automotive/Mobile Equipment Maintenance • Electrical & Electronics Repairer

Minimum ASVAB
56 in Mechanical for 2A5X2B • 51 in Mechanical for 2A5X2D

Security Clearance
Secret

Shred-outs
(B) H-60
(D) CV-22

THE TECH TO GUIDE OUR DEFENSES

2A5X3
Mobility Air Forces Electronic Warfare Systems

All Air Force aircraft are outfitted with sophisticated aviation technology to help guide their every move. It's the responsibility of Mobility Air Forces Electronic Warfare Systems specialists to maintain these systems to the highest standards. These experts go through extensive training to install and service radar, communications, weapons and other flight operations to ensure the safety of the aircraft and the crew and the successful completion of our missions.

Mobility Air Forces Electronic Warfare Systems specialists operate and maintain electronic warfare systems on C-5, C-17, C-130 and C-12 aircraft. They diagnose malfunctions utilizing schematics, wiring diagrams and other test equipment, and they prepare aircraft for low-altitude attack profiles and precision airdrops. They analyze and isolate malfunctions in avionics systems. They also establish methods and performance standards.

Requirements for this Career Field
Normal color • Completion of a current National Agency Check, Local Agency Checks and Credit

Relevant Interests & Skills
Computers & Computer Science • Electronics & Electrical • Weaponry & Materiel

Training Location
Sheppard AFB, TX for 100 days.

Related Civilian Careers
Aircraft Mechanic & Service Technician • Avionics Technician • Electrical and Electronics Installer and Repairer • Electronics Engineering Technician • Mechanical Engineering Technician

Minimum ASVAB
70 in Electrical

Security Clearance
Secret

Shred-outs
None

SAFETY THROUGH ESSENTIAL UPKEEP

2A5X4
Refuel / Bomber Aircraft Maintenance

Keeping our fleet refueled and our bombers ready to fly are monumental tasks. It's the job of the Refuel/Bomber Aircraft Maintenance specialists to inspect, troubleshoot and repair aircraft structures, engines and hydraulic systems. These professionals do everything from removing and installing engine components to identifying corrosion for prevention and repair to ensure that every time aircraft are in use they are safe and operating at full capacity.

Refuel / Bomber Aircraft Maintenance specialists utilize technical data to diagnose and solve maintenance problems on aircraft. They adjust, align and rig aircraft systems, and they inspect and check components for clearances, tolerances, proper installation, and operation. They inventory and maintain aircraft equipment. They also supervise the launching and recovery of aircraft.

Requirements for this Career Field
Normal color vision • Completion of a current National Agency Check, Local Agency Checks and Credit

Relevant Interests & Skills
Computers & Computer Science • Electronics & Electrical • Weaponry & Materiel

Training Location
Sheppard AFB, TX. Length varies with which aircraft being trained for.

Related Civilian Careers
Aircraft Mechanic & Service Technician • Inventory Management • Mechanical Engineering Technician • Industrial Machinery Mechanic • Electrical & Electronics Repairer • Maintenance & Repair Worker

Minimum ASVAB
47 in Mechanical

Security Clearance
Secret

Shred-outs
(A) Any C-135/E-3/E-8

(B) KC-10

(C) KC-46

(D) B-52

(E) B-1

(F) B-2

2A6X1
Aerospace Propulsion

It's imperative that our planes remain serviced so they can be ready to go at a moment's notice. Responsible for ensuring that all of our planes' engines are in first-rate operational conditions, Aerospace Propulsion specialists test, maintain and repair all parts of the engine. Bringing essential skill and knowledge to the flight line, these professionals play a critical part in keeping our planes and our Airmen safe in the air.

Aerospace Propulsion specialists plan, organize, and direct aerospace propulsion maintenance activities. They diagnose engine problems, including the fuel, oil, electrical and engine airflow systems. They remove defective components and install serviceable machinery, and they supervise test runs on repaired engines. They also analyze and recommend maintenance actions based on needs.

Requirements for this Career Field
Normal color vision • Completion of a current National Agency Check, Local Agency Checks and Credit

Relevant Interests & Skills
Aircraft & Flight • Maintenance & Repair

Training Location
Sheppard AFB, TX for 34 – 61 days.

Related Civilian Careers
Aircraft Mechanic & Service Technician • Aircraft Engine Mechanic • Industrial Machinery Mechanic • Inventory Management • Electronic Equipment Repairer

Minimum ASVAB
56 in Mechanical

Security Clearance
Secret

Shred-outs
(C) TF33, CF6, F103, F108, F117, TFE-731, TF34, TF39, PW 2040, F138 Jet Engines
(D) F100, F119, F135 Jet Engines
(E) F101, F110, F118 Jet Engines
(F) F100, F101, F110, F118, F119, F135 Jet Engines
(G) Turbofan and Turbojet Propulsion
(H) Turboprop and Turboshaft Propulsion

2A6X2
Aerospace Ground Equipment

When our planes aren't in the air, they're constantly receiving maintenance and being prepared for flight. Responsible for maintaining and repairing the equipment that supplies electricity, hydraulic pressure and air pressure to our planes, Aerospace Ground Equipment specialists play an essential role ensuring our planes are ready for flight. From inspecting and troubleshooting to making hands-on repairs and maintaining proper standards, these professionals make sure our planes are always ready for flight.

Aerospace Ground Equipment specialists perform necessary maintenance on aerospace ground equipment. They inspect and approve proper maintenance actions and they establish production controls and standards. They also determine equipment serviceability criteria when it doesn't exist.

Requirements for this Career Field
Normal color vision

Relevant Interests & Skills
Aircraft & Flight • Maintenance & Repair • Electronics & Electrical

Training Location
Sheppard AFB, TX for 95 days.

Related Civilian Careers
Heating, Air Conditioning, and Refrigeration • Maintenance and Repair • Automotive and Heavy Equipment Mechanic • Electronic Equipment • Fire and Hazardous Material • Hydraulic Equipment • Pneumatic Equipment

Minimum ASVAB
47 in Mechanical *and* 28 in Electrical

Security Clearance
None

Shred-outs
None

2A6X3
Aircrew Egress Systems

When a plane goes down, we have systems in place to prevent our Airmen from going with it. Responsible for maintaining all necessary exit equipment on our planes, Aircrew Egress Systems specialists ensure that pilots can safely eject from aircraft in the event of an emergency. By performing precise maintenance and coordination of seats, hatches, canopies and modules, these professionals make sure that every component is in perfect working order so that Airmen can make a safe escape when necessary.

Aircrew Egress Systems specialists handle and maintain explosive devices used to operate escape systems. They maintain and repair items associated with the escape and survival systems, and they diagnose malfunctions and recommend corrective action. They also perform scheduled and unscheduled maintenance on egress systems.

Requirements for this Career Field
Normal color vision

Relevant Interests & Skills
Maintenance & Repair

Training Location
Sheppard AFB, TX for 31 days.

Related Civilian Careers
Aircraft and Avionics Equipment Mechanic • Aircraft Structure, Surfaces, Rigging and Systems Assembler • Fire & Hazardous Material • Firearm Handling and Maintenance • Industrial Machinery Mechanic

Minimum ASVAB
56 in Mechanical

Security Clearance
None

Shred-outs
None

2A6X4
Aircraft Fuel Systems

There is little to no room for error during flight, especially when it comes to the fuel system. Responsible for diagnosing and repairing fuel system malfunctions, Aircraft Fuel Systems specialists correct problems before planes are airborne. By completing comprehensive checks on these complex systems, these highly trained specialists ensure that fuel systems won't malfunction during flight.

Aircraft Fuel Systems specialists inspect, repair and test aircraft hydraulic and in-flight refueling systems. They advise on aircraft fuel systems maintenance procedures and policies. They inspect fuel cells and tanks for foreign objects, corrosion, cell deterioration and fungus, and they maintain inspection and maintenance records. They recommend ways to improve equipment, performance and maintenance procedures. They also dispose of hazardous materials according to safety and environmentally acceptable standards.

Requirements for this Career Field
Normal color vision

Relevant Interests & Skills
Maintenance & Repair • Future Technologies • Aircraft & Flight

Training Location
Sheppard AFB, TX for 36 days.

Related Civilian Careers
Aircraft Mechanic & Service Technician • Fuel Handling & Distribution • Industrial Machinery Mechanic • Electrical & Electronics Repairer • Mechanical Engineering Technician • Maintenance & Repair Worker

Minimum ASVAB
47 in Mechanical

Security Clearance
None

Shred-outs
None

ENSURING CONTROLS STAY IN CONTROL

2A6X5
Aircraft Hydraulic Systems

Every part of our planes must be in perfect working order before we let them fly. Responsible for maintaining fluid-, air- or gas-pressured devices on aircraft, Aircraft Hydraulic Systems specialists ensure the hydraulic and pneumatic systems work as quickly and as efficiently as intended. Everything from landing gear and breaks to weapons and flight controls depend on the proper care and repair performed by these specialists.

Aircraft Hydraulic Systems specialists inspect the aircraft hydraulic systems, their components and any support equipment. They oversee malfunctions and advise on corrective action, and they maintain inspection and maintenance records. They also properly dispose of hazardous materials and waste.

Requirements for this Career Field
Normal color vision

Relevant Interests & Skills
Maintenance & Repair • Aircraft & Flight

Training Location
Sheppard AFB, TX for 49 days.

Related Civilian Careers
Aircraft Mechanic & Service Technician • Robotics Technician • Industrial Machinery Mechanic • Electrical & Electronics Repairer • Mechanical Engineering Technician • Maintenance & Repair Worker

Minimum ASVAB
56 in Mechanical

Security Clearance
None

Shred-outs
None

2A6X6
Aircraft Electrical and Environmental Systems

All of our aircraft rely on electricity and technology in order to work both safely and effectively. Responsible for maintaining and repairing the wiring and electrical components on an aircraft, Aircraft Electrical and Environmental Systems specialists make sure our planes are working at optimal condition. From cabin pressurization to engine control, these experts play a critical role keeping our aircraft and our Airmen safe and able to complete each mission.

Aircraft Electrical and Environmental Systems specialists inspect, troubleshoot and maintain electrical and environmental systems. They repair or replace any parts that are malfunctioning, and they perform cryogenic maintenance on mobile aircraft servicing units. They ensure compliance with technical publications and directives.

Requirements for this Career Field
Normal color vision

Relevant Interests & Skills
Electronics & Electrical • Future Technologies • Maintenance & Repair • Aircraft & Flight

Training Location
Sheppard AFB, TX for 91 days.

Related Civilian Careers
Aircraft Mechanic & Service Technician • Robotics Technician • Industrial Machinery Mechanic • Electrical & Electronics Repairer • Mechanical Engineering Technician • Maintenance & Repair Worker

Minimum ASVAB
41 in Mechanical *and* 61 in Electrical

Security Clearance
None

Shred-outs
None

CREATING PLANE COMPONENTS

2A7X1
Aircraft Metals Technology

Every part of a plane must be in perfect working order before we let them fly. Sometimes that even entails creating a part from scratch. Responsible for repairing and creating essential aircraft parts, Aircraft Metals Technology specialists act as the Air Force's machinists and welders. From troubleshooting to final fitting, these skilled professionals weld, fabricate and custom-make the metal components critical to the functioning of an aircraft.

Aircraft Metals Technology specialists measure broken or worn parts using calipers, gauges and micrometers. They draw working sketches, make templates, consult shop drawings and select materials. They perform precision grinding and remove poisonous or corrosive deposits. They also maintain and inspect hand tools and metal working machinery, and they write programs for machines using manual and computer-aided manufacturing methods.

Requirements for this Career Field
Normal depth perception

Relevant Interests & Skills
Electronics & Electrical • Maintenance & Repair • Aircraft & Flight

Training Location
Sheppard AFB, TX for 67 days.

Related Civilian Careers
Machinist • Welder, Cutter, Solderer & Brazer • Computer-Controlled Machine Tool Operator • Milling & Planing Machine Setter • Tool & Die Maker

Minimum ASVAB
47 in Mechanical

Security Clearance
None

Shred-outs
None

2A7X2
Nondestructive Inspection

No matter how well we maintain our equipment, wear and tear and metal fatigue can occur without visible signs. Responsible for employing noninvasive methods to inspect the insides of metal objects, Nondestructive Inspection specialists identify possible defects in systems and equipment before anything can become a dangerous problem. Utilizing everything from x-rays to ultrasound, these experts find the smallest imperfections and take the corrective measures needed to keep our equipment working safely.

Nondestructive Inspection specialists determine test methods and prepare fluids and parts for nondestructive inspection. They analyze wear metal content on engine lubricating oil and other fluids and recommend corrective action, and they detect flaws such as cracks, voids and heat damage utilizing various test equipment. They perform maintenance on shop equipment and tools, and handle and dispose of hazardous waste and materials.

Requirements for this Career Field
Normal color vision • Minimum age of 18 years prior to entry into technical training

Relevant Interests & Skills
Engineering & Applied Science • Future Technologies • Natural Science

Training Location
Pensacola NAS, FL for 49 days.

Related Civilian Careers
Non-Destructive Testing Specialist • Hazardous Materials Removal Worker • Chemical Equipment Operator • Gas Compressor Operator • Mechanical Engineering Technician

Minimum ASVAB
42 in Mechanical

Security Clearance
None

Shred-outs
None

2A7X3
Aircraft Structural Maintenance

When an aircraft suffers damage, it's essential to fix it and get back in the air. Responsible for repairing physical damage, Aircraft Structural Maintenance specialists maintain the high quality structures of Air Force aircraft. Utilizing various methods, these professionals do everything from installing replacement parts to building a replacement from scratch in order to restore the structural integrity of the aircraft and ensure the safety of the Airmen who fly them.

Aircraft Structural Maintenance specialists assess damage to aircraft and structural components and repair or replace necessary parts. They ensure all repairs are pressure-, fluid- and weather-tight, and they operate and maintain powered and non-powered tools and equipment. They remove corrosion by using various chemical and mechanical methods, and they form maintenance plans and policies to meet unit tasking. They also inspect structures and components to determine operational status.

Requirements for this Career Field
None

Relevant Interests & Skills
Aircraft & Flight • Maintenance & Repair

Training Location
Pensacola NAS, FL for 76 days.

Related Civilian Careers
Aircraft Mechanic & Service Technician • Sheet Metal Worker • Fire & Hazardous Material • Paint • Industrial Machinery Mechanic

Minimum ASVAB
47 in Mechanical

Security Clearance
None

Shred-outs
None

ENSURING OUR STEALTH EFFECT

2A7X5
Low Observable Aircraft Structural Maintenance

Advances in technology allow us to carry out aircraft missions without being detected, but it takes a skilled human touch to ensure the technology is properly in place. It's the job of Low Observable Aircraft Structural Maintenance specialists to design, fabricate and modify unique metals and bonded materials that create the stealth effect. From first application to repairing structural damage, these experts make sure aircraft can continually complete their missions completely undetected.

Low Observable Aircraft Structural Maintenance specialists apply low observable materials and coatings to aircraft, and they repair structural parts and components while preserving an aircraft's structural integrity. They determine the extent of damage to an aircraft and perform finishes and repairs accordingly, and they inspect final assembly to determine operational status. They also manufacture layouts, jigs, fixtures and molds.

Requirements for this Career Field
Completed and current (within the 5 years from the investigation close date) National Agency Check, Local Agency Checks and Credit

Relevant Interests & Skills
Aircraft & Flight • Maintenance & Repair

Training Location
Pensacola NAS, FL for 60 days.

Related Civilian Careers
Aircraft Mechanic & Service Technician • Robotics Technician • Mechanical Engineering Technician • Industrial Machinery Mechanic

Minimum ASVAB
47 in Mechanical

Security Clearance
Secret

Shred-outs
None

ADVANCING AIRCRAFT WITH ADVANCED TECH

2A8X1
Mobility Air Forces Integrated Communication / Navigation / Mission Systems

As the technology in our aircraft becomes more advanced, so does our need for more advanced and specialized care of all of our systems. It's the job of Mobility Air Forces Integrated Communication/Navigation/Mission Systems specialists to inspect, remove and install integrated avionics systems on our aircraft. From video display and electronic warfare systems to flight instruments and traffic-collision avoidance systems, these specialists ensure every system they work on works perfectly whenever it's needed.

These specialists operate and maintain communication, navigation and mission systems, and diagnose malfunctions using schematics and wiring diagrams. They inspect and verify operational status and configuration of avionics systems and software, and they establish methods and performance standards. They also supervise and assist in aircraft ground servicing and launch/recovery operations.

Requirements for this Career Field
Normal color vision • Completion of a current National Agency Check, Local Agency Checks and Credit

Relevant Interests & Skills
Aircraft & Flight • Computers & Computer Science • Electronics & Electrical

Training Location
Sheppard AFB, TX for 46 – 117 days.

Related Civilian Careers
Avionics Technician • Electrical Engineering Technician • Mechanical Engineering Technician • Electrical & Electronics Repairer • Manufacturing Production Technician

Minimum ASVAB
70 in Electrical

Security Clearance
Secret

Shred-outs
(A) C-5
(B) C-17
(C) C-130/WC-130 (except SOF/PR & EC-130)
(D) C-12/21/27/32/37/38/39/40
(E) Cargo Comm/Counter/Nav Systems
(F) KC-10
(G) KC-135
(H) KC-46
(J) Tanker Comm/Counter/Nav Systems

2A8X2
Mobility Air Forces Integrated Instrument and Flight Control Systems

The Air Force relies upon a wide array of aircraft to complete a variety of tasks integral to our mission. Specializing in electronics and avionics, Mobility Air Forces Integrated Instrument and Flight Control Systems specialists have a critical role keeping bombers, helicopters and cargo planes ready to go. These experts must keep everything to exacting standards to ensure systems operate as intended for the missions they complete all over the world.

These specialists operate and maintain instrument and flight control systems, and they perform maintenance on bombers, cargo aircraft, and helicopters. They diagnose malfunctions using technical orders, schematics, wiring diagrams, and test equipment. They interpret and recommend corrective action based on inspection findings, they establish methods and performance standards, and they also prepare aircraft for low-altitude attack profiles, precision bombing, covert operations, and reconnaissance.

Requirements for this Career Field
Normal color vision • Completion of a current National Agency Check, Local Agency Checks and Credit

Relevant Interests & Skills
Aircraft & Flight • Electronics & Electrical • Computers & Computer Science

Training Location
Sheppard AFB, TX for 46 - 95 days.

Related Civilian Careers
Avionics Technician • Electrical Engineering Technician • Mechanical Engineering Technician • Electrical & Electronics Repairer • Manufacturing Production Technician

Minimum ASVAB
70 in Electrical

Security Clearance
Secret

Shred-outs
(A) C-5
(B) C-17
(C) C-130/WC-130 (except SOF/PR & EC-130)
(D) C-12/21/27/32/37/38/39/40
(E) Cargo IFCS
(F) KC-10
(G) KC-135
(H) KC-46
(J) Tanker IFCS

MAINTAINING THE ABILITY TO FLY

2A9X1
Bomber / Special Integrated Communication / Navigation / Mission Systems

Keeping every system up and running on a bomber or specialty aircraft requires a lot of work. And often, the systems are essential to a mission's success. Responsible for installation, inspection, maintenance and repair, Bomber/Special Integrated Communication, Navigation and Mission Systems specialists ensure that the avionic systems under their care are in perfect working order and ready to go whenever the aircraft is needed.

These specialists operate and maintain communication/navigation systems on various aircraft, and they plan, organize and direct aircraft maintenance activities. They inspect and verify operational status of avionics systems, and they perform repairs and necessary updates to avionics systems as needed. They also establish performance standards and maintenance plans.

Requirements for this Career Field
Normal color vision •Completion of a current National Agency Check, Local Agency Checks and Credit

Relevant Interests & Skills
Aircraft & Flight • Electronics & Electrical • Computers & Computer Science • Maintenance & Repair

Training Location
Sheppard AFB, TX for 117 days.

Related Civilian Careers
Avionics Technician • Electrical Engineering Technician • Mechanical Engineering Technician • Electrical & Electronics Repairer • Manufacturing Production Technician

Minimum ASVAB
70 in Electrical

Security Clearance
Secret

Shred-outs
(A) E-3
(B) E-V/VC-25
(C) E-8
(D) RC-135
(E) B-1
(F) B-2
(G) B-52

2A9X2
Bomber / Special Integrated Instrument and Flight Control Systems

As technology advances, so does the way we fly our aircraft and complete our missions. Responsible for maintaining all aspects of flight controls, Bomber/Special Integrated Instrument and Flight Control Systems specialists ensure that every system in the cockpit operates without any flaws. These professionals review and analyze the instruments to make sure everything from GPS to in-flight warning systems meet exacting standards and perform perfectly whenever they're needed in the air.

These specialists operate and maintain instrument and flight control systems on various aircraft, and remove, install and repair avionics systems and line replaceable units. They inspect and evaluate aircraft maintenance activities, and interpret and recommend corrective action to inspection findings. They also establish maintenance methods and performance standards.

Requirements for this Career Field
Normal color vision • Completion of a current National Agency Check, Local Agency Checks and Credit

Relevant Interests & Skills
Aircraft & Flight • Electronics & Electrical • Computers & Computer Science • Maintenance & Repair

Training Location
Sheppard AFB, TX for 95 days.

Related Civilian Careers
Avionics Technician • Electrical Engineering Technician • Mechanical Engineering Technician • Electrical & Electronics Repairer • Manufacturing Production Technician

Minimum ASVAB
70 in Electrical

Security Clearance
Secret

Shred-outs
(A) E-3
(B) E-V/VC-25
(C) E-8
(D) RC-135
(E) B-1
(F) B-2
(G) B-52

2A9X3
Bomber / Special Electronic Warfare and Radar Surveillance Integrated Avionics

Pilots depend on highly advanced equipment to identify and locate all threats to their aircraft. It's the job of Bomber/Special Electronic Warfare and Radar Surveillance Integrated Avionics specialists to ensure these systems are maintained and remain in perfect working order. Responsible for everything from installation to repairs of a wide range of systems and equipment—including surveillance radar to video display systems—these professionals play an integral part in our mission success.

These specialists operate and maintain electronic warfare, radar surveillance and computer systems on various aircraft, and they also remove, install, check and repair avionics/computer systems and line replaceable units. They interpret and recommend corrective action to maintenance inspection findings, and they plan, organize and direct aircraft maintenance activities.

Requirements for this Career Field
Normal color vision • Completion of a current National Agency Check, Local Agency Checks and Credit

Relevant Interests & Skills
Aircraft & Flight • Electronics & Electrical • Computers & Computer Science

Training Location
Sheppard AFB, TX for 81 - 100 days.

Related Civilian Careers
Avionics Technician • Electrical Engineering Technician • Mechanical Engineering Technician • Electrical & Electronics Repairer • Manufacturing Production Technician

Minimum ASVAB
70 in Electrical

Security Clearance
Secret

Shred-outs
(A) E-3 Radar Surveillance
(B) E-3 Computer/Electronic Warfare System
(C) E-8
(D) RC-135/AFISRA Systems/Carry-on EW
(E) B-1
(F) B-2
(G) B-52
(H) EC-130 Compass Call
(J) VC-25

Fuels Careers(2F)

The Fuels career field encompasses operating, maintaining and managing petroleum fuel systems and activities including the entire spectrum of requisitioning, accounting, receiving, storing, dispensing, and testing of aviation and ground fuels, cryogenics, missile propellants and alternative fuels.

DISPENSING AIRCRAFT ENERGY

2F0X1
Fuels

Even with all of our advanced technology, our aircraft simply cannot operate without fuel. It is the job of Fuels specialists to manage every aspect of the refueling of every aircraft on the flight line. More than handling jet fuel, these professionals are also responsible for operating the vehicles, equipment and storage facilities that are essential to the refueling operation while also ensuring the compliance of all safety regulations while handling these volatile liquids.

Fuels specialists Maintain and operate fuels and cryogenic facilities and equipment, and they receive, store and issue petroleum products purchased for use in Air Force vehicles, aircraft and support equipment. They refuel aircraft with various types of mobile refueling equipment, they are responsible for the fuels control center, where all requests for fuel are received, and they conduct preventive maintenance inspections on the fuels vehicle fleet. They also maintain the bulk storage facility where millions of gallons of fuel are stored.

Requirements for this Career Field
Normal color vision • Must possess a valid state driver's license • Completion of a current National Agency Check, Local Agency Checks and Credit

Relevant Interests & Skills
Aircraft & Flight • Ground Vehicles • Logistics & Transportation

Training Location
Sheppard AFB, TX for 31 days.

Related Civilian Careers
Pump Operator • Chemical Plant & System Operator • Gas Compressor & Gas Pumping Station Operator • Separating, Filtering, Precipitating & Still Machine Setter

Minimum ASVAB
47 in Mechanical *and* 38 in General

Security Clearance
Secret

Shred-outs
None

Logistics Plans Careers(2G)

The Logistics Plans career field encompasses managing, administering, and operating logistics planning systems and activities supporting the expeditionary combat support principles of preparing the battle space, readying, positioning, employing, sustaining, and recovering the force.

2G0X1
Logistics Plans

Before any mission is carried out, a carefully thought out plan must be in place. Responsible for precise planning and organization, Logistics Plans specialists ensure that equipment and people are where they need to be when they need to be there. A crucial job, these experts consider all possible aspects, phases and contingencies while working in conjunction with other organizations to make sure every mission is safe, successful and goes according to their plan.

Logistics Plans specialists prepare, evaluate, and supervise all aspects of a mission's planning, and they provide planning support for associated units. They review planning documents to determine deployment tasking, and they develop crisis action procedures in conjunction with other employed organizations. They also maintain a close relationship between operations, logistics and support organizations.

Requirements for this Career Field
Ability to speak distinctly and communicate well with others • Ability to communicate effectively in writing • Completion of a current National Agency Check, Local Agency Checks and Credit

Relevant Interests & Skills
Arts & Humanity • Operations & Administration • Logistics & Transportation

Training Location
Lackland AFB, TX for 27 days.

Related Civilian Careers
Logistician • Transportation Manager • Purchasing Manager

Minimum ASVAB
56 in Administrative

Security Clearance
Secret

Shred-outs
None

Missile & Space Systems Maintenance Careers (2M)

The Missile and Space Systems Maintenance career field encompasses the skills, functions, and techniques used to acquire, activate, assemble, transport, install, and maintain missiles and subsystems.

2M0X1
Missile and Space Systems Electronic Maintenance

We work with some of the most advanced military technology on the planet. It takes an immense amount of skill and expertise to ensure everything remains in perfect working order. It's the responsibility of Missile and Space Systems Electronic Maintenance specialists to maintain and operate Air Force missiles, rockets and remotely piloted aircraft. These experts utilize critical skills to stay ahead of the latest technological advances and help us remain successful in our missions.

Missile and Space Systems Electronic Maintenance specialists monitor, operate, and supervise operation of consoles, fault display panels and checkout equipment. They monitor status of missiles, remotely piloted aircraft, boosters, payloads, and subsystems. They coordinate launch processing or maintenance activities, and they disassemble, inspect, service and replace components and wiring. They also design and supervise assembly of research and development systems.

Requirements for this Career Field
Screened for eligibility and meet requirements of the Personnel Reliability Program • Normal color vision • Qualification to operate government vehicles • Freedom from fear of heights • Completion of a Single Scope Background Investigation

Relevant Interests & Skills
Electronics & Electrical • Future Technologies • Maintenance & Repair • Space • Weaponry & Materiel • Computers & Computer Science

Training Location
Vandenburg AFB, CA for 59 days.

Related Civilian Careers
Computer, Automated Teller & Office Machine Repairer • Electrical & Electronics Repairer

Minimum ASVAB
70 in Electrical

Security Clearance
Top Secret

Shred-outs
(A) ICBM
(B) ALCM

2M0X2 – Missile and Space Systems Maintenance

Missiles and rockets are critical components of our national defense strategy. Responsible for servicing and maintaining them, Missile and Space Systems Maintenance specialists ensure these assets are fully operational at all times. From missile launchers to space lift boosters, these highly knowledgeable experts plan, organize and perform every service necessary to keep these systems in pristine working condition so they're ready when we need them.

Missile and Space Systems Maintenance specialists supervise and coordinate maintenance, operations and research and development functions. They perform preventive maintenance inspections and electrical tests on missiles, and they evaluate and direct missile maintenance, space lift booster and payload processing and R&D activities. They also interpret efficiency and equipment reliability findings and recommend improvements, and ensure compliance with international treaties relating to nuclear weapons and associated equipment.

Requirements for this Career Field
Screened for eligibility and meet requirements of the Personnel Reliability Program • Normal color vision • Qualification to operate government vehicles • Freedom from fear of heights • Completion of a Single Scope Background Investigation

Relevant Interests & Skills

Electronics & Electrical • Future Technologies • Maintenance & Repair • Space • Weaponry & Materiel • Computers & Computer Science

Training Location

Lackland AFB, TX for 70 days.

Related Civilian Careers

Computer, Automated Teller & Office Machine Repairer • Electrical & Electronics Repairer

Minimum ASVAB

47 in Mechanical

Security Clearance

Top Secret

Shred-outs

None

KEEPING US READY TO LAUNCH

2M0X3
Missile and Space Facilities

The intercontinental ballistic missile (ICBM) weapon system is one of our nation's most sophisticated and powerful defense tools. It's the responsibility of Missile and Space Facilities specialists to keep ICBM launch facilities at peak operational capability. Inspecting, maintaining, operating and repairing everything from launch control systems to facility heating and cooling systems, these professionals perform duties integral to keeping our country safe from attack.

Missile and Space Facilities specialists troubleshoot, repair, and service missile weapons system, and space lift equipment and facilities. They service support equipment, and they analyze support facility and equipment malfunctions to determine operational readiness. They also supervise space lift booster, payload systems maintenance, and launch processing, as well as perform inspections and operate special vehicles.

Requirements for this Career Field

Screened for eligibility and meet requirements of the Personnel Reliability Program • Normal color vision • Qualification to operate government vehicles • Freedom from fear of heights • Completion of a current National Agency Check, Local Agency Checks and Credit

Relevant Interests & Skills

Electronics & Electrical • Facilities • Maintenance & Repair • Space

Training Location
Vandenburg AFB, CA for 73 days.

Related Civilian Careers
Installation, Maintenance & Repair Worker • Geothermal Technician

Minimum ASVAB
70 in Electrical

Security Clearance
Secret

Shred-outs
None

Precision Measurement Equipment Laboratory Careers (2P)

The Precision Measurement Equipment Laboratory career field provides maintenance, modification, repair, calibration, and certification for test, measurement, and diagnostic equipment.

ENSURING EXACTING EQUIPMENT

2P0X1
Precision Measurement Equipment Laboratory

Any time a piece of equipment or machinery is used, there are an infinite number of things that need to work perfectly. Responsible for calibrating equipment used in virtually every phase of maintenance, Precision Measurement Equipment Laboratory specialists ensure that every piece of equipment is in precise working order. These experts must utilize exacting attention to detail as they take measurements in increments as small as millionths to ensure everything is safe for our Airmen to operate.

Precision Measurement Equipment Laboratory specialists repair, calibrate and modify test, measurement and diagnostic equipment. They record and report maintenance data and they provide training and manage technical order distributions. They develop workload plans and budget, and they also dispose of hazardous materials according to environmental standards.

Requirements for this Career Field
Normal color vision

Relevant Interests & Skills
Electronics & Electrical • Engineering & Applied Science • Maintenance & Repair • Computers & Computer Science

Training Location
Keesler AFB, MS for 124 days.

Related Civilian Careers
Precision Instrument & Equipment Repairer

Minimum ASVAB
70 in Electrical

Security Clearance
None

Shred-outs
None

Maintenance Management Careers (2R)

The Maintenance Management Systems career field includes planning and scheduling aircraft, missiles, and associated equipment.

2R0X1
Maintenance Management Analysis

The Air Force must maintain tens of thousands of pieces of equipment in support of our missions and daily operations. And all of our maintenance activities must operate within fixed budgets and defined schedules. It's the responsibility of Maintenance Management Analysis specialists to determine the cost efficiency of these activities. These professionals collect and analyze data and report their findings and recommendations for improvement up the chain of command to ensure our operations run as efficiently as possible.

Maintenance Management Analysis specialists monitor maintenance performance data systems for compliance with established procedures, and they audit deficiencies in areas such as equipment performance, scheduling and resources. They manage and operate maintenance on management information systems. They also prepare oral and written presentations to keep managers informed of unit progress, and they identify and assist in analysis and study of materiel deficiencies, man-hours costs and trends and deviations from standards.

Requirements for this Career Field
Completion of a current National Agency Check, Local Agency Checks and Credit

Relevant Interests & Skills
Operations & Administration • Maintenance & Repair • Computers & Computer Science

Training Location
Sheppard AFB, TX for 56 days.

Related Civilian Careers
Production, Planning & Expediting Clerk • Procurement Clerk • Cargo & Freight Agent • Dispatcher • Secretary & Administrative Assistant

Minimum ASVAB
55 in General

Security Clearance
Secret

Shred-outs
None

ENSURING CONSTANT MACHINERY UPKEEP

2R1X1
Maintenance Management Production

From aircraft and missiles to refueling trucks and jet engines, there's no shortage of machines that require maintenance in the Air Force. Ensuring that all the equipment is regularly maintained is the job of Maintenance Management Production specialists. These professionals work with crew chiefs and mechanics to plan, schedule and organize aerospace vehicle maintenance to make sure all of our equipment and machinery is always ready and working whenever it's needed.

Maintenance Management Production specialists develop plans and create production schedules to meet mission requirements, and they ensure that all maintenance requirements and operational commitments are met. They also maintain historical records for weapons and support systems, and they schedule maintenance jobs, establish work priorities and monitor completion.

Requirements for this Career Field
Completion of a current National Agency Check, Local Agency Checks and Credit

Relevant Interests & Skills
Operations & Administration • Maintenance & Repair • Computers & Computer Science

Training Location
Sheppard AFB, TX for 33 days.

Related Civilian Careers
Production, Planning & Expediting Clerk • Procurement Clerk • Cargo & Freight Agent • Dispatcher • Secretary & Administrative Assistant

Minimum ASVAB
44 in General

Security Clearance
Secret

Shred-outs
None

Materiel Management Careers (2S)

The Materiel Management career field encompasses managing, controlling, and operating materiel management systems associated with specified Classes of Supply.

2S0X1
Materiel Management

No matter what their position is, every Airman needs equipment and supplies to do their job. Responsible for managing inventory, Materiel Management specialists administer and operate complex supply systems to ensure financial accountability for all of the utilized supplies. An incredibly detailed and critical job, these specialists ensure every asset—from paperclips to multimillion-dollar machinery—is accounted for and where it needs to be whenever our Airmen need them.

Materiel Management specialists are responsible for demand processing and mission support, and they manage, administer and operate supply systems and activities in order to provide the necessary equipment and supplies for Air Force operations. They perform item and monetary accounting and inventory stock control, they plan and schedule material storage and distribution activities, and they prevent unauthorized changes of information to the materiel management system database. They also control and operate the Remote Processing Station.

Requirements for this Career Field
None

Relevant Interests & Skills
Operations & Administration • Computers & Computer Science

Training Location
Lackland AFB, TX for 33 days.

Related Civilian Careers
Shipping, Receiving & Traffic Clerk • Stock Clerk • Order Filler, Wholesale & Retail Sales • Weigher, Measurer & Sampler • Inspector, Tester & Sorter

Minimum ASVAB
41 in Administrative *or* 44 in General

Security Clearance
None

Shred-outs
None

Transportation & Vehicle Management Careers (2T)

The Transportation and Vehicle Management career field encompasses transportation functions involving traffic management, air transportation, ground transportation and vehicle management.

2T0X1
Traffic Management

From paper clips to helicopters, the Air Force ships millions of dollars' worth of equipment and supplies around the world every year. It's the responsibility of Traffic Management specialists to manage the transportation of personnel and their dependents, material and property as they travel from base to base. A vital job that requires great attention to detail, these experts keep track of every shipment in order to ensure everything gets into the right hands at the right time.

Traffic Management specialists ensure that shipments are ready for transport, and assist personnel and dependents with their personal property movements. They prepare transportation requests and authorizations and arrange for quality-control visits to personal property pickup sites. They select and arrange official travel for individuals and groups and also schedule proper carrier equipment for loading and unloading.

Requirements for this Career Field
Must possess a valid state driver's license • Must maintain ability to ship, transport, possess, or receive firearms or ammunition • Completion of a current National Agency Check, Local Agency Checks and Credit

Relevant Interests & Skills
Operations & Administration • Logistics & Transportation • Computers & Computer Science

Training Location
Ft. Lee, VA for 44 days.

Related Civilian Careers
Cargo & Freight Agent • Bill & Account Collector • Customer Service Representative • Dispatcher • Insurance Policy Processing Clerk

Minimum ASVAB
35 in Administrative

Security Clearance
Secret

Shred-outs
None

2T1X1
Ground Transportation

Many Air Force operations depend upon ground vehicles in order to complete many aspects of their mission. It's the responsibility of Ground Transportation specialists to transport people, supplies, munitions and outsized expeditionary forces. These professionals must utilize a variety of essential skills, such as map and compass reading, vehicle specifications determination and limitations assessment in order to coordinate and master all aspects of ground transportation necessary for us to get equipment and people where they need to go.

Ground Transportation specialists operate, service, and perform preventative maintenance on government motor vehicles. They conduct pre- and post-operation vehicle inspections, and they provide transportation services for distinguished visitors and special events. They coordinate and schedule cargo movement, they conduct night operations, including operating vehicles in blackout conditions, and they also investigate accidents or incidents.

Requirements for this Career Field
Must possess a valid state driver's license • Must maintain eligibility to deploy and mobilize worldwide • Normal color vision

Relevant Interests & Skills
Ground Vehicles

Training Location
Ft. Leonard Wood, MO for 30 days.

Related Civilian Careers
Heavy & Tractor-Trailer Truck Driver • Locomotive Firer • Railroad Brake, Signal & Switch Operator • Motorboat Operator • Delivery Services Driver

Minimum ASVAB
40 in Mechanical

Security Clearance
None

Shred-outs
None

2T2X1
Air Transportation

In order to provide our bases with the resources they need, we must control a lot of moving parts. Responsible for securely managing cargo and passengers, Air Transportation specialists ensure that everything and everyone on a military aircraft is transported safely and quickly. From food and medical supplies to helicopters and ground vehicles, these professionals are responsible for coordinating the valuable people and supplies we ship around the world.

Air Transportation specialists perform and manage air transportation activities, and they inspect aircraft cargo to verify proper documentation, packaging and marking. They determine quantity and type of cargo to be loaded according to allowable aircraft cabin load, and they implement necessary safety and security precautions for handling and storing dangerous materials. They also load and unload aircraft using specialized equipment, and provide the Department of Defense with the capability to move air passengers and cargo worldwide.

Requirements for this Career Field
Must possess a valid state driver's license

Relevant Interests & Skills
Aircraft & Flight • Logistics & Transportation • Ground Vehicles

Training Location
Ft. Lee, VA for 29 days.

Related Civilian Careers
Cargo & Freight Agent • Bill & Account Collector • Customer Service Representative • Receptionist & Information Clerk • Insurance Policy Processing Clerk

Minimum ASVAB
47 in Mechanical *and* 28 in Administrative

Security Clearance
None

Shred-outs
None

KEEPING OUR FLEET MOVING

2T3X1
Mission Generation Vehicular Equipment Maintenance

The Air Force utilizes a wide range of vehicles that require a wide range of maintenance needs. Responsible for inspecting and troubleshooting vehicle repairs, Mission Generation Vehicular Equipment Maintenance specialists make sure that every vehicle on the base remains in working order. From snow blowers and dump trucks to forklifts and cranes, these experts are trained to service every system on every vehicle so our base operations can continue running smoothly.

Mission Generation Vehicular Equipment Maintenance specialists perform vehicle maintenance activities on military vehicles and equipment, and determine the overall mechanical condition of vehicles and equipment. They remove and install electrical components to facilitate repairs, they perform preventative maintenance and special inspections, and they properly handle the disposal of hazardous waste.

Requirements for this Career Field
Normal color vision • Must possess a valid state driver's license

Relevant Interests & Skills
Electronics & Electrical • Maintenance & Repair • Ground Vehicles

Training Location
Port Heuneme, CA for 79 days.

Related Civilian Careers
Automotive Master Mechanic • Bus & Truck Mechanic & Diesel Engine Specialist • Mobile Heavy Equipment Mechanic

Minimum ASVAB
47 in Mechanical for 2T3X1 • 40 in Mechanical for 2T3X1A and 2T3X1C

Security Clearance
None

Shred-outs
(A) Firefighting and Refueling Vehicle & Equipment Maintenance
(C) Material Handling Equipment (MHE)/463L Maintenance

2T3X7
Fleet Management and Analysis

The Air Force utilizes thousands of vehicles for our operations that all require unique maintenance demands. It's the job of Fleet Management and Analysis specialists to keep every vehicle in our motor pool up and running. These professionals utilize the latest computer technology to keep track of the maintenance schedules as well as forecasting the long-term needs of every vehicle on base to ensure that the vehicles are always running when they're needed.

Fleet Management and Analysis specialists supervise and perform the scheduling and analysis of maintenance performed on vehicles and equipment. They oversee fleet management and accounts for vehicle fleet, they file historical data and maintain vehicle records, and they coordinate with work center supervisors to ensure timely repair of vehicles. They also monitor and coordinate vehicles on military construction projects.

Requirements for this Career Field
None

Relevant Interests & Skills
Operations & Administration • Computers & Computer Science • Ground Vehicles

Training Location
Lackland AFB, TX for 33 days.

Related Civilian Careers
Logistician • Transportation Manager • Purchasing Manager

Minimum ASVAB
41 in Administrative

Security Clearance
None

Shred-outs
None

Munitions & Weapons Careers (2W)

The Munitions and Weapons career field includes assembling, maintaining, storing, delivering, inventory management, and loading nonnuclear munitions and solid propellants; and handling and aircraft loading nuclear munitions and guided aircraft missiles and rockets.

2W0X1
Munitions Systems

As a superior military force, we work with some of the most advanced weapons in the world. It's the great responsibility of Munitions Systems specialists to assemble and process nonnuclear munitions. Working with a high level of attention to detail and extreme care, these experts handle, store, transport, arm and disarm weapons systems to ensure the safety of our Airmen and the success of our missions.

Munitions Systems specialists receive, identify, inspect, store, recondition, ship, issue, deliver, maintain, test and assemble guided and unguided non-nuclear munitions. They handle, store, and transport weapons and locally dispose of nonhazardous unserviceable munitions. They prepare munitions for loading on aircraft, inspect munitions for serviceability, and they conduct inventories and correct discrepancies. They also establish and evaluate performance standards, maintenance controls and work procedures.

Requirements for this Career Field
Normal color vision • No record of emotional instability • Normal depth perception • Must possess a valid state driver's license • Never been convicted of domestic violence • Completion of a current National Agency Check, Local Agency Checks and Credit

Relevant Interests & Skills
Aircraft & Flight • Maintenance & Repair • Ground Vehicles • Weaponry & Materiel • Electronics & Electrical

Training Location
Sheppard AFB, TX for 43 days.

Related Civilian Careers
Explosives Worker, Ordnance Handling Expert & Blaster • Maintenance & Repair Worker • Hazardous Materials Removal Worker • Rotary Drill Operator

Minimum ASVAB
60 in Mechanical

Security Clearance
Secret

Shred-outs
None

ENSURING EXPLOSIVES CAN DROP

2W1X1
Aircraft Armament Systems

When a mission involves dropping explosive devices, everything needs to be in perfect working order. Responsible for maintaining launch and release devices on aircraft, Aircraft Armament Systems specialists ensure that explosive devices can be accurately delivered from our planes. From testing and evaluating new weapons systems to loading ordnance, these professionals make sure that when a pilot pulls the trigger, the devices successfully launch away from the aircraft toward the target.

Aircraft Armament Systems specialists load, unload, and position munitions on aircraft, and they operationally check and electrically test aircraft weapons release and gun systems. They remove, disassemble, and inspect parts that might be damaged, and they perform armament systems maintenance functions. They also participate in the test and evaluation of new and prototype weapons and weapons systems.

Requirements for this Career Field
No record of emotional instability • Normal depth perception • Normal color vision • Completion of a current National Agency Check, Local Agency Checks and Credit

Relevant Interests & Skills
Aircraft & Flight • Maintenance & Repair • Weaponry & Materiel • Electronics & Electrical

Training Location
Sheppard AFB, TX for 45 - 86 days.

Related Civilian Careers
Explosives Worker, Ordnance Handling Expert & Blaster • Maintenance & Repair Worker • Hazardous Materials Removal Worker • Rotary Drill Operator

Minimum ASVAB
60 in Mechanical

Security Clearance
Secret

Shred-outs
(C) A-10
(E) F-15
(F) F-16
(J) F-35
(K) B-52/B-2
(L) B-1
(N) F-22
(Q) RPA (MQ-1/MQ-9)
(Z) All Other

2W2X1
Nuclear Weapons

As a superior military force, the Air Force maintains and occasionally utilizes superior nuclear weapons systems. It's the responsibility of Nuclear Weapons specialists to inspect, store and repair these weapons and associated equipment. Utilizing extreme attention to detail, these highly trained experts work with our incredibly diverse nuclear arsenal to ensure that these delicate materials remain safe, stable and secure until the exact moment they're needed to support our national defense.

Nuclear Weapons specialists inspect, assemble, disassemble, maintain, repair, refinish, modify and test nuclear warheads, bombs, missiles, reentry vehicles and systems and associated equipment. They Comply with nuclear safety measures, and they resolve maintenance problems and submit deficiency reports on faulty components. They also assist in performing operational checks on alarm systems, and perform escort duties.

Requirements for this Career Field
Normal color vision • Normal depth perception • Must possess a valid state driver's license • Never been convicted of domestic violence • Must be screened for eligibility and meet requirements of the Personnel Reliability • No record of emotional instability • Completion of a current Single Scope Background Investigation

Relevant Interests & Skills
Future Technologies • Maintenance & Repair • Weaponry & Materiel • Natural Science

Training Location
Sheppard AFB, TX for 67 days.

Related Civilian Careers
Explosives Worker, Ordnance Handling Expert & Blaster • Maintenance & Repair Worker • Hazardous Materials Removal Worker • Rotary Drill Operator

Minimum ASVAB
60 in Mechanical

Security Clearance
Top Secret

Shred-outs
None

Cyberspace Support Careers (3D)

The Cyberspace Support career field encompasses Knowledge Operations Management, Cyber Systems Operations, Cyber Surety, and Computer Systems Programming. Included are activities to: plan, coordinate, share, and control an organization's data and information assets and manage technologies to capture, organize, and store tacit and explicit knowledge.

3D0X1
Knowledge Operations Management

The one tool more powerful than missiles is the information used to launch them. Responsible for the coordination and distribution of information and data, Knowledge Management specialists play a critical role in every department of the Air Force. From creating launch manuals to storing and disposing of high-level documents, these professionals manage the flow, distribution, life cycle and disposal of communications and information integral to our operations.

Knowledge Operations Management specialists manage the process for coordination, management and control of information, and they identify and analyze data. They develop, plan, and integrate base communications systems. They also assist and educate users on authoritative data sources, data services and presentation tools, as well as evaluate contracts, contingency and exercise plans to determine impact on manpower, equipment and systems.

Requirements for this Career Field
None

Relevant Interests & Skills
Operations & Administration • Computers & Computer Science

Training Location
Keesler AFB, MS for 41 days.

Related Civilian Careers
Document Management Specialist • Desktop Publisher

Minimum ASVAB
64 in General

Security Clearance
None

Shred-outs
None

3D0X2
Cyber Systems Operations

The Air Force relies heavily on advanced computer and software systems, so it is paramount to keep those systems safe. It's the job of Cyber Systems Operations specialists to design, install and support our systems to ensure they operate properly and remain secure from outside intrusion. These experts enhance our capabilities and provide us with the best and most secure systems so we can stay ahead of the curve in everything we do.

Cyber Systems Operations specialists install, support, and maintain servers or other computer systems, and they ensure current defensive mechanisms are in place. They respond to service outages and interruptions to network operations, they perform strategic and budget planning for systems hardware and software, and they support information warfare operations within strictly controlled parameters.

Requirements for this Career Field
Must attain and maintain a minimum Information Assurance Technical Level II • Completion of a current Single Scope Background Investigation

Relevant Interests & Skills
Intelligence • Computers & Computer Science

Training Location
Keesler AFB, MS for 66 days.

Related Civilian Careers
Network & Computer Systems Administrator • Computer Systems Analyst • Database Administrator • Computer Network Architect • Computer Systems Engineer

Minimum ASVAB
64 in General *or* 54 in General *and* 60 on Cyber-Test

Security Clearance
Top Secret

Shred-outs
None

PROTECTING OUR INFORMATION

3D0X3
Cyber Surety

The continued advancement of computers and technology has drastically expanded our capabilities. However, these very same advancements have created vulnerability to our security as well. Responsible for preventing, detecting and repelling cyber attacks, Cyber Surety specialists ensure the security of computer networks and online communications. From programming to hardware, these experts keep our systems and our information safe.

Cyber Surety specialists are responsible for cyber-security of national security systems. They monitor, evaluate and maintain systems, policy and procedures to protect networks and systems from unauthorized activity. They identify and repel any potential threats or attempts at unauthorized access into networks, and they enforce national, Department of Defense, and Air Force security policies and directives. They also ensure all systems comply with national security standards.

Requirements for this Career Field
Must attain and maintain a minimum Information Assurance Management Level I • Completion of a current Single Scope Background Investigation

Relevant Interests & Skills
Intelligence • Computers & Computer Science

Training Location
Keesler AFB, MS for 50 days.

Related Civilian Careers
Information Security Analyst • Logistics Analyst • Computer Systems Analyst • Software Developer • Computer Network Architect • Computer Systems Engineer

Minimum ASVAB
64 in General *or* 54 in General *and* 60 on Cyber-Test

Security Clearance
Top Secret

Shred-outs
None

3D0X4
Computer Systems Programming

The Air Force employs countless computers to accomplish each mission. But a computer is only as good as its software, which is where Computer Systems Programming specialists come in. These experts write, analyze, design and develop programs that are critical to our war-fighting capabilities. From maintenance tracking programs to programs that organize and display intelligence data, they ensure we have the software and programs needed to complete our missions efficiently and effectively.

Computer Systems Programming specialists develop standardized tools and interfaces in accordance with Air Force Network, and they provide operations guidance to transform raw data into actionable command and control information. They protect operating systems, software files, and databases from unauthorized access, and they determine, analyze and develop requirements for software systems. They also conduct test events and maintain test data, as well as develop and prepare system requirements and proposals.

Requirements for this Career Field
A minimum score of 71 on the Air Force Electronic Data Processing Test • Completion of a current Single Scope Background Investigation

Relevant Interests & Skills
Computers & Computer Science

Training Location
Keesler AFB, MS for 70 days.

Related Civilian Careers
Computer Programmer • Computer Systems Analyst • Software Developer • Database Administrator

Minimum ASVAB
64 in General *or* 54 in General *and* 60 on Cyber-Test

Security Clearance
Top Secret

Shred-outs
None

PROVIDING TECHNOLOGICAL SUPPORT

3D1X1
Client Systems

Computers and technology continue to be an integral part of everything we do. Providing the Air Force with communications networking expertise, Client Systems specialists ensure that all of our computer hardware and software function correctly at all times. From installing necessary programs to troubleshooting and repairing any problems that arise, these experts play a critical role ensuring that we maintain the access and control of the technology necessary to complete all of our missions.

Client Systems specialists install and configure software operating systems and applications, they perform information technology support functions, and they establish preventive, scheduled and unscheduled maintenance actions. They report security incidents and takes corrective measures, and they also integrate base communications systems.

Requirements for this Career Field
Must possess a valid state driver's license • Normal color vision • Must attain and maintain a minimum Information Assurance Technical Level II certification • Completion of a current National Agency Check, Local Agency Checks and Credit

Relevant Interests & Skills
Computers & Computer Science • Future Technologies

Training Location
Keesler AFB, MS for 67 days.

Related Civilian Careers
Computer, Automated Teller & Office Machine Repairer • Computer User Support Specialist • Electrical Engineering Technician • Audio & Video Equipment Technician

Minimum ASVAB
60 in Electrical *or* 55 in Electrical *and* 60 on Cyber-Test

Security Clearance
Secret

Shred-outs
None

PROVIDING COMMUNICATION THROUGH CONNECTION

3D1X2
Cyber Transport Systems

A vast, global communications network is one of the many things that makes us the most powerful air force on the planet. Making sure the underlying infrastructure of this network is operating properly is the responsibility of Cyber Transport Systems specialists. Whether it's repairing a network hub at a stateside base or installing fiber-optic cable at a forward installation overseas, these experts keep our communications systems up and running and play an integral role in our continuing success.

Cyber Transport Systems specialists upgrade and replace systems and circuits, and they deploy, sustain, troubleshoot, and repair standard voice, data and video network infrastructure systems and cryptographic equipment. They analyze capabilities and performance, identify problems, and take corrective action. They also apply communication security programs.

Requirements for this Career Field
Normal color vision • Must possess a valid state driver's license • Must attain and maintain a minimum Information Assurance Technical Level II certification • Completion of a current Single Scope Background Investigation required for (R) shred-out

Relevant Interests & Skills
Computers & Computer Science • Future Technologies

Training Location
Keesler AFB, MS for 136 days.

Related Civilian Careers
Telecommunications Engineering Specialist

Minimum ASVAB
70 in Electrical *or* 60 in Electrical *and* 60 on Cyber-Test

Security Clearance
Top Secret

Shred-outs:
(R) Data Links

3D1X3
Radio Frequency (RF) Transmission Systems

Communication is essential to our base operations and the effective pursuit of our missions. It's the job of Radio Frequency Transmission Systems specialists to install and maintain our radio frequency communications. These experts must deploy, sustain, troubleshoot and repair the vast variety of communications devices—including antenna systems, tuners and transmission lines—to ensure our ability to communicate and our continued success.

RF Transmission Systems specialists perform wireless radio and satellite systems and equipment maintenance activities, and they deploy and activate mobile and transportable transmission equipment. They determine equipment operational status, they install ground radio, satellite, and telemetry communication systems, and they also evaluate base comprehensive plan and civil engineering projects.

Requirements for this Career Field
Normal color vision • Completion of a current National Agency Check, Local Agency Checks and Credit

Relevant Interests & Skills
Computers & Computer Science • Electronics & Electrical

Training Location
Keesler AFB, MS for 96 days.

Related Civilian Careers

Communications Equipment Operator

Minimum ASVAB

70 in Electrical

Security Clearance

Secret

Shred-outs

None

KEEPING US CONNECTED

3D1X7
Cable and Antenna Systems

Effective communication is vital to any mission's success, so it's essential we have the means to do so. It's the job of Cable and Antenna Systems specialists to ensure that all cable and wireless systems are installed and maintained. From Local Area Networks (LANs) and Wide Area Networks (WANs) to coaxial cable and antenna systems, these experts make sure that we maintain the ability to monitor a mission and communicate with our Airmen from anywhere in the world.

Cable and Antenna Systems specialists install, maintain and modify copper core, coaxial, waveguide and fiber-optic cable and antenna systems. They climb antenna support structures and wooden poles to various heights for maintenance, and they interpret technical data to work on cable and antenna systems. They operate and perform maintenance on tools, test equipment, auxiliary equipment and vehicles. They also locate, repair, and replace faulty closures in various systems.

Requirements for this Career Field
Normal color vision • Must possess a valid state driver's license • Normal depth perception • Normal gait and balance • Physical ability to perform climbing duties • Freedom from fear of heights and claustrophobia

Relevant Interests & Skills
Maintenance & Repair • Electronics & Electrical

Training Location
Sheppard AFB, TX for 80 days.

Related Civilian Careers
Electrical Power-Line Installer & Repairer • Maintenance & Repair Worker

Minimum ASVAB
55 in Mechanical *or* 55 in Electrical

Security Clearance
None

Shred-outs
None

Civil Engineering Careers (3E)

The Civil Engineering career field encompasses mechanical and electrical activities, structural and pavement activities, utilities systems, fire protection, Explosive Ordnance Disposal, and Readiness activities.

3E0X1
Electrical Systems

Every Air Force base and installation around the world requires electricity to operate successfully. Responsible for installing, repairing and maintaining this electrical network, Electrical Systems specialists ensure that our primary source of energy is always available. From space command communicating with our satellites to hospitals operating lifesaving equipment, every Air Force function depends on this crucial service provided by these experts.

Electrical Systems specialists install, service, modify, and repair electrical equipment and systems. They troubleshoot malfunctions and recommend necessary repair procedures, and they install and maintain airfield lighting systems. They also survey proposed work to determine resource requirements.

Requirements for this Career Field
Must possess a valid state driver's license • Freedom from fear of heights • Normal color vision

Relevant Interests & Skills
Facilities • Electronics & Electrical

Training Location
Sheppard AFB, TX for 99 days.

Related Civilian Careers
Electrician • Heating & Air Conditioning Mechanic & Installer

Minimum ASVAB
35 in Mechanical *and* 35 in Electrical

Security Clearance
None

Shred-outs
None

POWERING OUR OPERATIONS

3E0X2
Electrical Power Production

From hangars and control towers to tents and temporary disaster relief centers, electricity is paramount to everything we do. It's the job of Electrical Power Production specialists to ensure that we always have electricity readily available. These experts utilize a vast array of skills and knowledge to do everything from starting up portable generators to maintaining and operating power stations to keep all of our bases operating at full capacity.

Electrical Power Production specialists determine operational readiness of power production equipment, check installed equipment to ensure compliance with policies, and they operate high- and low-voltage switches, circuit breakers and other controls. They interpret maintenance-malfunction data and electrical wiring diagrams, and they identify, troubleshoot and repair defective power-generating components. They also advise on projects associated with electrical power-generating and control systems.

Requirements for this Career Field
Must possess a valid state driver's • Normal color vision

Relevant Interests & Skills
Facilities • Electronics & Electrical • Maintenance & Repair

Training Location
Sheppard AFB, TX for 55 days.

Related Civilian Careers
Stationary Engineer & Boiler Operator • Control & Valve Installer & Repairer • Maintenance & Repair Worker • Gas Plant Operator

Minimum ASVAB
56 in Mechanical *and* 40 in Electrical

Security Clearance
None

Shred-outs
None

IN CONTROL OF COMFORT

3E1X1
Heating, Ventilation, Air Conditioning, and Refrigeration

Climate control plays a large role in the comfort and efficiency of our Airmen as well as our electronic equipment. Responsible for maintaining the mechanical systems that keep our surroundings temperature-controlled, Heating, Ventilation, Air Conditioning and Refrigeration (HVAC/R) specialists ensure that every space at their respective base is functioning correctly. These experts install, maintain and repair the different HVAC/R systems necessary for us to complete our operations in a variety of climates all over the world.

HVAC/R specialists install, maintain and operate heating, ventilation, air conditioning and refrigeration systems and equipment. They perform recurring maintenance and seasonal overhaul on every system, and solve maintenance problems through use of wiring, schematic drawings and analyzing construction. They also survey proposed work to determine resource requirements.

Requirements for this Career Field
Normal color vision • Must possess a valid state driver's license

Relevant Interests & Skills
Facilities • Electronics & Electrical

Training Location
Sheppard AFB, TX for 98 days.

Related Civilian Careers
Refrigeration Mechanic & Installer • Electrician • Elevator Installer & Repairer • Heating & Air Conditioning Mechanic & Installer

Minimum ASVAB
47 in Mechanical *or* 28 in Electrical

Security Clearance
None

Shred-outs
None

3E2X1
Pavements and Construction Equipment

Our ability to extend our presence and worldwide impact is due to our ability to have working bases wherever we're needed. It's the great responsibility of Pavements and Construction Equipment personnel to construct runways and airfields in remote global locations in addition to maintaining facilities already in use. These professionals are part of a team that does everything from operating heavy construction equipment to detonating explosives in order to care for and create the facilities we need most.

Pavements and Construction Equipment specialists operate and maintain heavy construction equipment, and construct, maintain and inspect concrete and asphalt runways, aircraft parking aprons and roads. They schedule and coordinate equipment repair and servicing, and they inspect work to ensure quality and compliance with policies. They also design demolition projects, place and detonate explosives.

Requirements for this Career Field
Normal color vision • Must possess a valid state driver's license

Relevant Interests & Skills
Facilities • Natural Science • Ground Vehicles

Training Location
Ft. Leonard Wood, MO for 69 days.

Related Civilian Careers

Paving, Surfacing, and Tamping Equipment Operator • Cement Mason & Concrete Finisher • Pile-Driver Operator • Highway Maintenance Worker • Rail-Track Laying and Maintenance Equipment Operator • Excavating & Loading Machine Operator

Minimum ASVAB

40 in Mechanical

Security Clearance

None

Shred-outs

None

3E3X1
Structural

The buildings and structures on each base are integral to every part of Air Force operations. It's the job of Structural Specialists to construct and repair any buildings and other structures from the foundation up. These highly trained experts use their varied skill sets and specialized materials, tools and equipment to build anything we need, from improvised emergency disaster relief shelters to locker rooms.

Structural specialists construct, maintain, plan and repair wooden, masonry and concrete buildings and structures, including concrete footings, foundations, walls, floor slabs, piers and columns. They lay structures according to blueprints, building plans and other directives. They install interior and exterior trim and finishing materials. They repair and install manufactured locking devices and erect scaffolding and work from ladders and mobile platforms. They also ensure compliance with environmental regulations.

Requirements for this Career Field
Normal color vision • Must possess a valid state driver's license • Freedom from fear of heights.

Relevant Interests & Skills
Engineering & Applied Science • Facilities

Training Location
Gulfport, MS for 90 days.

Related Civilian Careers
Brickmason & Blockmason • Construction Carpenter • Cement Mason & Concrete Finisher • Structural Iron & Steel Worker

Minimum ASVAB
47 in Mechanical

Security Clearance
None

Shred-outs
None

3E4X1
Water and Fuel Systems Maintenance

The Air Force must maintain thousands of miles of fuel and water lines essential to our daily operations. It's the job of Water and Fuel Systems Maintenance specialists to manage the plumbing, wastewater collection systems, liquid fuel storage and natural gas distribution systems on every base. These professionals are highly trained in a wide variety of areas, including the principles of operation and construction and fire suppression systems in order to keep our bases running smoothly while upholding the highest environmental standards.

Water and Fuel Systems Maintenance specialists install and maintain all water, natural gas and fire suppression systems. They monitor systems operation to compliance with local, state, federal and DoD regulations. They install and operate field potable water treatment equipment, and they remove, repair and replace defective system components. They also analyze water to determine water purification treatment methods, and survey proposed facility work to determine resource requirements.

Requirements for this Career Field
Must possess a valid state driver's license • Freedom from fear of confined spaces • Freedom from fear of heights • Normal color vision

Relevant Interests & Skills
Aircraft & Flight • Logistics & Transportation • Maintenance & Repair

Training Location
Sheppard AFB, TX for 86 days.

Related Civilian Careers
Water & Wastewater Treatment Plant and System Operator • Stationary Engineer & Boiler Operator • Electrical & Electronics Repairer

Minimum ASVAB
47 in Mechanical *and* 28 in Electrical

Security Clearance
None

Shred-outs
None

3E4X3
Pest Management

They may seem harmless, but insects, rodents and birds can significantly impair the operations on any Air Force base. It's the responsibility of Pest Management specialists to take the necessary actions to control and prevent pest infestations. These professionals do everything from keeping bases free of pests that could carry debilitating infectious diseases to repelling birds from airfields to ensure safe takeoff and landings, protecting the health and safety of everyone on base.

Pest Management specialists Conduct pest management surveys, determine actions needed to control and prevent infestations of plant and animal pests, and ensure compliance with laws and directives. They maintain tools, equipment, facilities, and storage areas, as well as evaluate proposed work to determine resource and cost estimates.

Requirements for this Career Field
No record of entomophobia (fear of insects, spiders, etc.), ophiciophobia (fear of snakes), zoophobia (fear of animals) and claustrophobia (fear of confined spaces), or hypersensitivity to chemicals or arthropod (insect, spider, scorpion, etc.) and snake venoms • Freedom from fear of heights • Normal color vision

Relevant Interests & Skills
Facilities • Natural Science

Training Location
Sheppard AFB, TX for 33 days.

Related Civilian Careers
Pest Control • Occupational Health & Safety Technician • Animal Control • Environmental Engineering Technician

Minimum ASVAB
38 in General

Security Clearance
None

Shred-outs
None

3E5X1
Engineering

From roads to buildings, when something needs to be constructed on an Air Force base, it needs to be done with skill and precision. Responsible for planning and managing construction projects, Engineering specialists ensure that every base has the facilities and structures they need to keep operating successfully. With tasks that include surveying, computer-aided drafting and soil testing, these highly trained experts make sure that every project operates smoothly and without any unforeseen problems.

Engineering specialists conduct reconnaissance, site location, construction and mapping surveys. They develop, operate, and maintain Geographic Information System (GIS) modules, and they evaluate potential construction sites. They manage and inspect construction and maintenance contracts, they transform rough sketch ideas into accurate construction drawings and specifications, and they also develop plans to beddown personnel, aircraft, and associated support functions during contingency operations.

Requirements for this Career Field
Must possess a valid state driver's license • Normal color vision

Relevant Interests & Skills
Facilities • Engineering & Applied Science

Training Location
Ft. Leonard Wood, MO for 71 days.

Related Civilian Careers
Civil Engineering Technician • Civil Drafter • Electrical Drafter • Mapping Technician • Power Distributor

Minimum ASVAB
49 in General

Security Clearance
None

Shred-outs
None

OVERSEEING A PROJECT'S EVERY DETAIL

3E6X1
Operations Management

The Air Force constructs and maintains thousands of facilities around the world, and keeping these projects on time and under budget is not an easy task. It's the responsibility of Operations Management specialists to manage projects from start to finish, ensuring schedules are met, materials are available and everything stays within budget. These experts coordinate details with a large number of people, including engineers, civilian contractors and other vendors to make sure the job gets done right.

Operations Management specialists manage the operation of command and control systems and customer focal points, and they develop, monitor and manage work order priority program. They monitor work costs to ensure compliance with legal limits or support agreements, they manage and ensure a continuous workflow, and they ensure all environmental concerns are being addressed. They also analyze work activities to ensure compliance with Air Force policies.

Requirements for this Career Field
Must possess a valid state driver's license • Ability to speak clearly, concisely, and distinctly

Relevant Interests & Skills
Operations & Administration • Logistics & Transportation

Training Location
Sheppard AFB, TX for 28 - 43 days.

Related Civilian Careers
Business Operations Specialist • Dispatcher

Minimum ASVAB
44 in General

Security Clearance
None

Shred-outs
None

3E7X1
Fire Protection

The Air Force operates with unusual materials and unique environments all over the world, so we need specialists prepared for anything. Acting as the firemen of the Air Force, Fire Protection specialists deal with everything from brush fires to burning rocket fuel and hazardous material fires. Upholding our mission to ensure the safety of others, these specialists don't just act on Air Force bases, but assist civilian fire departments when needed as well.

Fire Protection specialists Protect people, property, and the environment from fires and disasters, and they provide fire prevention guidance. They manage and operate fire alarm communication centers, they operate specialized equipment to help control fire outbreak, and they establish public relations and conduct fire prevention awareness and educational training. They also administer emergency first aid Preserve and protect emergency scene evidence.

Requirements for this Career Field
No record of pyrophobia, acrophobia, or claustrophobia • Ability to speak distinctly • Must possess a valid state driver's license • Normal color vision • Must meet physical standards • Completion of a current National Agency Check, Local Agency Checks and Credit

Relevant Interests & Skills
Emergency Management & Response • Health & Medicine

Training Location
Goodfellow AFB, TX for 68 days.

Related Civilian Careers
Firefighter

Minimum ASVAB
38 in General

Security Clearance
Secret

Shred-outs
None

3E8X1
Explosive Ordnance Disposal (EOD)

Trained to detect, disarm, detonate and dispose of explosive threats all over the world, EODs are the specialists who bravely serve as the Air Force's bomb squad. Assigned to some of the most dangerous missions, they perform tactically harrowing and technically demanding tasks in diverse environments worldwide. A job for the best and bravest, they do what needs to be done to keep others safe.

EOD specialists handle explosives daily, and they detect, identify, recover, disarm and dispose of unsafe explosives and ordnance. They conduct nuclear weapon response, and maintain equipment, technical data and vehicles. They analyze unknown munitions and explosives for intelligence agencies, as well as provide protection to the president, vice president and other dignitaries.

Requirements for this Career Field
Minimum height of 5'2" • Maximum height 6'8" • No record of Claustrophobia • Minimum score of 30 required on EOD selection model • Must pass two components of the EOD Physical Ability and Stamina Test • No record of emotional instability • Normal depth perception • Normal color vision • Single Scope Background Investigation due to training, assignments involving nuclear weapons and Presidential support

Relevant Interests & Skills
Emergency Management & Response • Electronics & Electrical • Future Technologies • Weaponry & Materiel • Facilities

Training Location
Sheppard AFB, TX; and Eglin AFB, FL for 169 days.

Related Civilian Careers
Explosives Worker • Ordnance Handling Expert & Blaster • Firefighter • Hazardous Materials Removal Worker • Rotary Drill Operator

Minimum ASVAB
60 in Mechanical *and* 64 in General

Security Clearance
Secret

Shred-outs
None

3E9X1
Emergency Management

Whether it's a natural disaster (tornados, hurricanes, etc.) or man-made as a result of a chemical, biological, radiological or nuclear incident, Emergency Management specialists are trained for response and recovery operations anywhere in the world. Additionally, these professionals develop plans to ensure all other Air Force personnel are trained to meet mission needs and to minimize casualties and damage in the event of any disaster situation.

Emergency Management specialists protect personnel from the effects caused by incidents involving weapons of mass destruction, and perform advanced training exercises and disaster simulations. They also develop emergency response plans to ensure the safety of fellow Airmen.

Requirements for this Career Field
Ability to speak distinctly • Normal color vision • Must possess a valid state driver's license • No record of claustrophobia or claustrophobic tendencies • Completion of a current National Agency Check, Local Agency Checks and Credit

Relevant Interests & Skills
Emergency Management & Response • Natural Science • Health & Medicine • Operations & Administration

Training Location
Ft. Leonard Wood, MO for 67 - 500 days.

Related Civilian Careers
Business Continuity Planner

Minimum ASVAB
62 in General

Security Clearance
Secret

Shred-outs
None

Force Support Careers (3F)

The Force Support career field sustains and builds ready and resilient Airmen with a wide array of installation support functions, including personnel, military equal opportunity, education and training, manpower, administration, and services.

3F0X1
Personnel

Our most valued assets are our Airmen, and their growth and career development is one of our top priorities. Advising on job specialties, promotions and training programs, Personnel specialists give Airmen the counsel and resources they need to help them achieve their long-term career goals. These experts also provide essential information regarding benefits and duty assignments, ensuring that our Airmen are fully informed about all aspects of their service and growth.

Personnel specialists assist and counsel military personnel and dependents on matters that concern them in the Air Force community, and they create, maintain and audit personnel records of military members. They conduct interviews to determine individual interests and qualifications, and they monitor retention programs and provide reports and statistics. They oversee personnel activities and functions, they ensure compliance with personnel policies, directives and procedures, and they also conduct in-and-out processing.

Requirements for this Career Field
None

Relevant Interests & Skills
Arts & Humanity • Operations & Administration

Training Location
Keesler AFB, MS for 26 days.

Related Civilian Careers
Human Resources Assistant • Office Clerk • Tax Examiner & Collector • Paralegal & Legal Assistant • Secretary

Minimum ASVAB
41 in Administrative

Security Clearance
None

Shred-outs
None

3F1X1
Services

It takes all types of Airmen to perform duties necessary to keep our bases operational. It's the job of Services specialists to maintain and operate hotels, restaurants and fitness centers at bases all over the world. These experts perform a variety of tasks; from conducting physical fitness tests to helping families relocate to new bases in order to support their fellow Airmen and keep our operations running smoothly.

Services specialists manage and direct Force Support programs, operations and retail operations. They establish and supervise facilities that provide food, lodging and sports among others, and they manage a budget for a variety of services. They determine effectiveness of service and retail operation programs. They promote physical fitness to maintain Air Force unit readiness and coordinate with commanders to ensure readiness of unit.

Requirements for this Career Field
Ability to speak distinctly • Never been convicted by courts-martial • Never been convicted and sentenced to confinement by a civilian court • No record of disciplinary action for financial irresponsibility, shoplifting, larceny, petty larceny, or theft.

Relevant Interests & Skills
Operations & Administration • Health & Medicine • Arts & Humanity

Training Location
Ft. Lee, VA for 29 days.

Related Civilian Careers
Cook • Recreation Worker • Retail Salesperson • Hotel, Motel, and Resort Desk Clerk

Minimum ASVAB
24 in General

Security Clearance
None

Shred-outs
None

MAKING EVERY DAY EFFICIENT

3F5X1
Administration

To perform to our high standards, we must have the proper support at every level. Responsible for coordinating and managing a variety of tasks and activities, Administration Airmen work directly with directors and leaders to help with their daily workload. From human resources and managing calendars to arranging travel and preparing official documents, these diligent professionals ensure that every day the Air Force is working to its highest efficiency.

Administration specialists provide administrative support to Air Force, Department of Defense and joint organizations. They ensure communications comply with proper standards for style and format, and they coordinate with Protocol and assist with welcoming Distinguished Visitors. They also perform postal services and maintain appropriate records.

Requirements for this Career Field
None

Relevant Interests & Skills
Operations & Administration

Training Location
Keesler AFB, MS for 41 days.

Related Civilian Careers
Human Resources Assistant • Postal Service Clerk • Secretary • Administrative Assistant

Minimum ASVAB
47 in Administrative

Security Clearance
None

Shred-outs
None

Public Affairs Careers (3N)

The Public Affairs career field serves the United States Air Force by providing professional, trained communication practitioners to leaders and managers for planning, training, executing, and reporting.

3N0X2
Broadcast Journalist

Radio and television are powerful tools for telling and preserving the Air Force story. Responsible for the recording, documenting and producing of radio and television material, Broadcast Journalists represent and communicate the interests of the Air Force. These specialists have a wide array of responsibilities and do everything from writing and editing copy and serving as on-camera announcers to maintaining the archive library to ensure information is saved for future generations.

Broadcast Journalists supervise broadcast radio and television programming, perform documentation and maintain archive library, and operate the latest media technology–editing software. They also produce news and information products to support mission requirements, and establish relationship with local and regional news media.

Requirements for this Career Field
A favorable evaluation of a voice audition • Absence of any speech impediment • Ability to read aloud and speak distinctly • Must possess a valid state driver's license • Normal color vision • Completion of a current National Agency Check, Local Agency Checks and Credit

Relevant Interests & Skills
Arts & Humanity • Computers & Computer Science

Training Location
Ft. Meade, MD for 77 days.

Related Civilian Careers
Radio & T.V. Announcer • Broadcast Technician • Reporter & Correspondent • Copy Writer • Film & Video Editor

Minimum ASVAB
72 in General

Security Clearance
Secret

Shred-outs
None

3N0X5 Photojournalist

Telling the Air Force story to a global audience requires captivating and informative communication. It's the job of Photojournalists to shape and maintain the public image of the Air Force. More than just providing photos, these experts work with commanders and media operations to write and manage content for our website, social media and various periodicals in order to ensure our many accomplishments are told in the most appropriate light possible.

Photojournalist specialists prepare and release news and imagery for internal and public audiences, they conduct research and interview subject matter experts, and they document joint operations, exercises and contingencies for internal and external use. They respond to media queries and facilitate interviews, they maintain liaison with local and regional government and civic leaders, and they perform investigative and medical photo documentation.

Requirements for this Career Field
Ability to type 20 words per minute • Normal color vision • Absence of any speech impediment • Ability to read aloud and speak distinctly • Completion of a current National Agency Check, Local Agency Checks and Credit • Must possess a valid state driver's license

Relevant Interests & Skills
Arts & Humanity

Training Location
Ft. Meade, MD for 60 days.

Related Civilian Careers
Public Relations Specialist • Advertising & Promotions Manager • Market Research Analyst • Copy Writer

Minimum ASVAB
72 in General

Security Clearance
Secret

Shred-outs
None

3N1X1
Regional Band

The Air Force is proud of our Airmen, our mission and our role in defending our country. One of the best ways to display this is through music played by Air Force bands all over the country. Vocalists, percussionists, electric guitarists, pianists, brass, woodwind players, music arrangers and sound engineers all work together as members of Regional Bands to rehearse and perform various events to celebrate and honor the men, women and efforts of the U.S. Air Force.

The Regional Band performs events in various regions throughout the United States, they arrange and adapt music for various musical combinations, and they coordinate activities with interested agencies and higher authorities (Musicians). They perform one or more musical instrument in concert, marching bands and other musical groups, and they also prep facilities for rehearsals and performances.

Requirements for this Career Field
None

Relevant Interests & Skills
Arts & Humanity

Training Location
N/A

Related Civilian Careers
Musician • Self-Enrichment Education Teacher • Teacher Assistant • Singer • Radio & T.V. Announcer • Tour Guide & Escort

Minimum ASVAB
21 in Administrative *or* 24 in General

Security Clearance
None

Shred-outs
(A) Clarinet
(B) Saxophone
(C) Bassoon
(D) Oboe
(E) Flute & Piccolo
(F) Horn
(G) Cornet & Trumpet
(H) Baritone & Euphonium
(J) Trombone
(K) Tuba
(L) Percussion
(M) Piano
(N) Guitar
(P) Music Arranger
(Q) Bagpipe
(R) Vocalist
(S) Electric Bass/String Bass
(U) Steel Guitar
(V) Audio and Light Engineer
(Z) Instrumentalist, General (Air National Guard Bands)

ELITE TALENT, PREEMINENT PRIDE

3N2X1
Premier Band

One of the many ways we share our Air Force pride is through music. The U.S. Air Force Band is composed of some of our nation's finest musicians. The only Premier Band in the Air Force, these talented specialists utilize their talents in support of official military, recruiting and community outreach events. Vocalists, percussionists, string players, pianists, woodwind instruments and sound engineers all work together to bring patriotism and ceremony to events all around the world.

The Premier Band performs in and with various ensembles throughout the United States and around the world, they coordinate activities such as concerts, parades and rehearsals, and they arrange and adapt music for various musical combinations. They audition personnel for promotional and training purposes, and they complete minor maintenance on musical equipment.

Requirements for this Career Field
Prior qualification in and possession of AFSC 3N151X, or prior qualification as a musician • Completion of a current National Agency Check, Local Agency Checks and Credit

Relevant Interests & Skills
Arts & Humanity

Training Location
N/A

Related Civilian Careers
Singer • Musician • Radio & T.V. Announcer • Actor • Tour Guide & Escort

Minimum ASVAB
21 in Administrative *or* 24 in General

Security Clearance
Secret

Shred-outs
None

Security Forces Careers (3P)

The Security Forces career field performs force protection duties, which require use of force, up to and including the use of deadly force. Security Forces duties ensure combat capability through the functions of installation security, nuclear and conventional weapon systems and resources security, air base defense, law enforcement, information security, military working dog activities, and combat arms training and maintenance.

3P0X1
Security Forces

An important part of protecting our country is ensuring the safety of the people, property and resources on every Air Force base. To accomplish this goal, Security Forces specialists go through extensive training in law enforcement and combat tactics to protect bases both stateside and overseas. A job that's both physically and mentally demanding, these highly focused experts do everything from writing tickets to investigating on-base incidents to make sure everyone and everything on every base is protected.

Security Forces specialists ensure the safety of all base weapons, property and personnel. They conduct investigations into any on-base incidents, and they participate in team patrol movements, tactical drills, battle procedures and military operations other than war. They apprehend and detain suspects, secure crime scenes and testify in judicial proceedings. They apply life saving procedures as first responders to disaster scenes, and they also train handlers and military working dogs.

Requirements for this Career Field

Normal color vision • No history of excessive alcohol use • Must not have used a substance to obtain an altered conscious state • No more than one active wage garnishment for delinquency • No more than two delinquent charge off/collection (>= 30 days) payments within last two years • Not have been terminated from civilian employment more than twice for reasons of misconduct, theft, or alcohol use within past three years • No record of sleep disorders • No current diagnosis of ADD/ADHD in the last 12 months • No history of Bipolar Disorders, Depressive Disorders, or Anxiety Disorders • No history of emotional instability • Distance visual acuity correctable to 20/20 in one eye and 20/30 in the other • Qualification for arming, suitability to arm • Never been diagnosed with a severe substance use disorder • No speech disorder • Individuals who have had their spleen removed are not eligible for assignment to the military working dog program • Must possess a valid state driver's license • No diagnosed fear of fear of heights or confined spaces • No documented record of gang affiliation • No fear working around nuclear weapons or components, nor have an identifiable negative opinion of the role of nuclear weapons in our nation's strategic deterrent mission • Must not have used/distributed/manufactured illicit narcotics • Never failed prescribed rehabilitation program where alcohol use is concerned • Completion of a current National Agency Check, Local Agency Checks and Credit

Relevant Interests & Skills
Emergency Management & Response • Law & Enforcement • Weaponry & Materiel

Training Location
Lackland AFB, TX for 65 days.

Related Civilian Careers
Police Patrol Officer • Correctional Officer & Jailer • Police Detective • Criminal Investigator • Transit & Railroad Police

Minimum ASVAB
33 in General for 3P0X1 and 3P0X1A • 35 in Mechanical for 3P0X1B

Security Clearance
Secret

Shred-outs
(A) Military Working Dog Handler
(B) Combat Arms

Medical Careers (4 Except 4Y)

The Civil Engineering career field encompasses mechanical and electrical activities, structural and pavement activities, utilities systems, fire protection, Explosive Ordnance Disposal, and Readiness activities.

KEEPING HEALTHCARE OPERATING

4A0X1
Health Services Management

It takes more than doctors and nurses to keep our Air Force medical facilities up and running. Responsible for handling everything leading up to and following patient visits, Health Services Management specialists keep all our medical facilities operating efficiently. These professionals' skills are called upon to do everything from processing patient records and administering facilities to coordinating payments and preparing staffing plans, ensuring that every patient can get the top-rate care they need when they need it.

Health Services Management specialists provide administrative support to the entire hospital staff, they file and maintain inpatient and outpatient medical records, and perform and manage financial statements, budget estimates and financial plans. They use medical computer systems for patient scheduling, budgeting and staffing, they interview patients for admission and discharge purposes, and they monitor information technology security programs. They also analyze and advise on the completeness and accuracy of healthcare data.

Requirements for this Career Field
None

Relevant Interests & Skills
Operations & Administration • Computers & Computer Science • Health & Medicine • Health Technicians & Specialists • Health Administration

Training Location
Ft. Sam Houston, TX for 36 days.

Related Civilian Careers
Medical Records & Health Information Technician • Receptionist • Medical Secretary • Office Clerk

Minimum ASVAB
44 in General

Security Clearance
None

Shred-outs
None

4A1X1
Medical Materiel

It's essential that our medical teams have all of the tools needed to provide proper care and treatment. It's the job of Medical Materiel specialists to ensure that all Air Force medical facilities have the medications, supplies and equipment they need to treat our Airmen and their families. These experts order, receive and store these supplies, making certain that every facility has what they need, precisely when they need it.

Medical Materiel specialists order and receive medical and nonmedical supplies and equipment from government and civilian sources for your medical treatment facility. They establish stock control levels and inventory control, they analyze reports and records and take necessary corrective action, and they monitor expenses and funds. They also perform inventories of all stock maintained in storage areas.

Requirements for this Career Field
Must possess a valid state driver's license

Relevant Interests & Skills
Operations & Administration • Health & Medicine • Health Technicians & Specialists • Logistics & Transportation

Training Location
Ft. Sam Houston, TX for 24 days.

Related Civilian Careers
Stock Clerk • Warehouse

Minimum ASVAB
44 in General

Security Clearance
None

Shred-outs
None

4A2X1
Biomedical Equipment

With today's technology, providing top-notch healthcare means having top-rate equipment. So when medical devices need repairing and/or replacing, it's the job of Biomedical Equipment specialists to fix the problem. From replacing parts and repairing components to inspecting equipment to ensure they fall within operating regulations, these professionals play a critical part in keeping our hospitals and field clinics fully operational.

Biomedical Equipment specialists install, repair, and modify biomedical equipment and support systems. They inspect biomedical equipment systems to ensure they comply with technical standards and specifications. They develop new procedures to be implemented for maintenance activities, and they perform preventive maintenance and safety inspections. They also manage facility management programs.

Requirements for this Career Field
Normal color vision • Minimum age of 18 years prior to technical training

Relevant Interests & Skills
Electronics & Electrical • Health & Medicine • Health Technicians & Specialists • Maintenance & Repair

Training Location
Ft. Sam Houston, TX for 207 days.

Related Civilian Careers
Medical Equipment Repairer • Robotics Technician • Electrical & Electronics Repairer

Minimum ASVAB
60 in Mechanical *and* 70 in Electrical

Security Clearance
None

Shred-outs
None

4B0X1
Bioenvironmental Engineering (BE)

Life in the Air Force takes our Airmen to a variety of facilities and environments all over the world. It's the job of Bioenvironmental Engineering specialists to focus on reducing health hazards in the workplace and the surrounding areas. A job complicated by the proximity to everything from munitions to radioactive materials, these experts utilize their skills to ensure healthful working conditions and that the environment is not adversely affected by Air Force activities.

BE specialists conduct preventive medicine studies and provide recommendations to reduce health risk to personnel, and they identify health hazards as well as potable and non-potable water sources. They execute Occupational & Environmental Health Site Assessments, and they respond to terrorist attacks, natural disasters or accidents which may result in exposure to health threats. They also conduct examinations to reduce health risk or negative impact in future operations, and advise senior leadership and affected communities on health risks associated with operations and missions.

Requirements for this Career Field

No record of acrophobia or claustrophobia • Ability to speak distinctly • Must possess a valid state driver's license • Normal color vision • Normal depth perception • Ability to wear a 40-pound air pack while carrying 40 pounds of equipment in a totally encapsulating chemical protective suit • Be medically qualified

Relevant Interests & Skills
Engineering & Applied Science • Health & Medicine • Health Technicians & Specialists • Natural Science • Applied Health

Training Location
Wright Patterson AFB, OH for 68 days.

Related Civilian Careers
Occupational Health & Safety Technician • Environmental Compliance Inspector • Industrial Safety & Health Engineer • Product Safety Engineer • Soil & Water Conservationist

Minimum ASVAB
49 in General

Security Clearance
None

Shred-outs
None

4C0X1
Mental Health Service

The challenges of working in the Air Force can be both physically and mentally taxing. Working with psychiatrists and psychologists, Mental Health Service specialists are responsible for ensuring that every Airman is mentally fit. These experts help evaluate and provide mental healthcare to patients around the world to help them overcome mental obstacles and issues so they can get back to their job, their lives and their mission.

Mental Health Service specialists perform initial basic assessment to obtain a patient's clinical information, administer and score psychological tests, and they assist patients with nutritional, hygiene and comfort measures. They explain and interpret mental health services to patients and others, they perform combat and disaster casualty care procedures, and they compile and prepare medical and administrative reports.

Requirements for this Career Field

Must complete the Minnesota Multiphasic Personality Inventory assessment • Must undergo a standardized entry interview • No history of psychiatric hospitalization • No evidence of emotional instability, impulsive behaviors or misconduct that is contrary to the standards of the mental health and substance abuse counseling profession • No history or evidence of personality disorder, substance use disorder, or other significant disorders • No evidence or history of civilian conviction, as a result of illicit drug or alcohol use, driving under the influence/impaired, financial irresponsibility, promiscuity, physical or sexual assault or misconduct, or domestic violence • No evidence or history of disruptive conduct, behavior, attitude, or communication as a result of prejudice, discrimination, harassment, threats, or reprisal • Must possess the ability to read aloud and speak distinctly • No unresolved mental health problems • No record of ethical misconduct or violations

Relevant Interests & Skills
Mental Health • Health & Medicine • Health Technicians & Specialists

Training Location
Ft. Sam Houston, TX for 66 days.

Related Civilian Careers
Psychiatric Technician • Social & Human Services • Occupational Therapy Assistant • Physical Therapist Assistant • Correctional Officer & Jailer

Minimum ASVAB
55 in General

Security Clearance
None

Shred-outs
None

MENDING HEALTH THROUGH NUTRITION

4D0X1
Diet Therapy

There are many things that can help speed the recovery of our sick or injured Airmen. Responsible for helping patients heal and stay healthy through nutrition, Diet Therapy specialists plan and prepare meals for the needs of everyone they treat. From leading classes on how to maintain health through diet to assembling patient trays, these experts ensure that our Airmen not only get healthy, but remain that way.

Diet Therapy specialists select nourishment for regular and therapeutic diets, establish production controls and standards for quantity and quality of foods, and they receive and process diet orders and menus. They calculate simple, routine therapeutic diets, and they also assist in determining requirements for local purchase orders.

Requirements for this Career Field
None

Relevant Interests & Skills
Natural Sciences • Health & Medicine • Health Technicians & Specialists • Allied Health

Training Location
Ft. Sam Houston, TX for 33 days.

Related Civilian Careers
Cooks, Institution & Cafeteria • Dietetic Technician • Baker • Butcher • Food Preparation & Serving

Minimum ASVAB
44 in General

Security Clearance
None

Shred-outs
None

4E0X1
Public Health

Whether they're active in the field or performing duties on base, the safety of our Airmen is a top priority. It's the job of Public Health specialists to protect our forces from a vast array of illness and disease by minimizing health risks within our community. Responsible for everything from educating Airmen on safety procedures and food inspection to investigating hazardous materials and sanitary standards, these professionals perform public health activities ensuring that our Airmen remain healthy on bases all over the world.

Public Health specialists control disease transmission through patient interviews, investigations and community outreach programs. They conduct food safety and defense programs, they assess risks associated with production, transportation, storage, preparation and serving of food, and they advise healthcare providers on workplace hazards. They also oversee medical clearances for deploying personnel.

Requirements for this Career Field
Normal color vision • Hearing Conservation certification is mandatory • Must pass Reading Aloud Test • Valid state driver's license

Relevant Interests & Skills
Natural Science • Health & Medicine • Health Technicians & Specialists • Allied Health

Training Location
Wright Patterson AFB, OH for 47 days.

Related Civilian Careers
Occupational Health & Safety Technician • Environmental Engineering Technician • Fire Inspector • Agricultural Inspector • Construction & Building Inspector

Minimum ASVAB
44 in General

Security Clearance
None

Shred-outs
None

4H0X1
Cardiopulmonary Laboratory

Caring for our Airmen and their families requires the knowledge and skills of thousands of individuals. Assisting doctors who diagnose and treat diseases of the heart and lungs, Cardiopulmonary Laboratory specialists perform essential lab and clinical functions to help care for their patients. From conducting blood tests, electrocardiograms and ultrasounds to assisting with surgical procedures, these highly trained professionals help prevent, monitor and minimize heart and lung disease within the Air Force.

Cardiopulmonary Laboratory specialists work with doctors and other health professionals in the diagnosis and treatment of diseases of the heart and lungs. They perform pulmonary diagnostic studies, electrocardiograms, and ultrasound tests, and they assist in long-term respiratory therapy, including the use of sophisticated life-support equipment to assist patients in breathing. They also draw blood from patients to perform necessary blood tests, and assist in catheterization and other special studies of the heart.

Requirements for this Career Field

Must possess a current Certified Respiratory Therapist (or higher level Respiratory Therapy) credential from the National Board of Respiratory Care • Must possess a current Certified Cardiographic Technologist credential from the Cardiovascular Credentialing International • Must remain proficient and current in Respiratory Therapy

Relevant Interests & Skills
Natural Science • Health & Medicine • Health Technicians & Specialists

Training Location
Ft. Sam Houston, TX for 233 days.

Related Civilian Careers
Cardiovascular Technician • Radiation Therapist • Respiratory Therapist • Diagnostic Medical Sonographer • Nuclear Medicine Technician

Minimum ASVAB
44 in General

Security Clearance
None

Shred-outs
None

4J0X2
Physical Medicine

When an Airman is injured or wounded, we do everything we can to help them get back on their feet. Working hand in hand with Physical Therapists, Physical Medicine specialists help patients recover from muscle and bone problems. These experts implement exercise programs and treatments that fulfill a vital role in helping injured Airmen make a full recovery.

Physical Medicine specialists assist Physical Therapists with patient evaluations and tests, and fabricate splints and aid devices to protect and assist patients. They observe and record patient responses to treatment, manage material and equipment, and provide quality patient care in an ethical, safe, sanitary and caring environment.

Requirements for this Career Field
None

Relevant Interests & Skills
Natural Science • Health & Medicine • Health Technicians & Specialists

Training Location
Ft. Sam Houston, TX for 81 days.

Related Civilian Careers
Physical Therapist Assistant • Registered Nurse • Psychiatric Technician • Occupational Therapy Assistant • Medical Assistant

Minimum ASVAB
62 in General *or* 49 in General *and* 60 on Cyber-Test

Security Clearance
None

Shred-outs
(A) Orthotic

4M0X1
Aerospace and Operational Physiology

When Airmen are flying at 50,000 feet, they have to be prepared for every situation. Responsible for teaching pilots and aircrews the essential skills they need to handle in-flight emergencies, Aerospace and Operational Physiologists prepare our Airmen for the most extreme circumstances before they ever set foot on a plane. Additionally, these professionals conduct training on proper pre- and postflight preparation and even participate in high-altitude missions to ensure the health and safety of our flying Airmen.

Aerospace and Operational Physiology specialists provide pilots and crew members with the necessary skills to handle emergencies, and schedule and operate low-pressure chambers to simulate the experience of flying. They supervise and ensure safe operation of physiological training devices and proper health of participants, and they conduct lectures, discussions and demonstrations to showcase the physiological stresses. They participate in parachuting activities when assigned. They also maintain records on use of the hypobaric chambers and the effects of participants, and resolve technical problems pertaining to aerospace and operational physiology activities.

Requirements for this Career Field
Ability to speak clearly and distinctly without speech impediments • Physical qualification for aerospace and operational physiology duty

Relevant Interests & Skills
Natural Science • Health & Medicine • Allied Health

Training Location
Wright Patterson AFB, OH for 42 days.

Related Civilian Careers
Health Technician

Minimum ASVAB
44 in General

Security Clearance
None

Shred-outs
None

4N0X1
Aerospace Medical Service

The hundreds of medical facilities we have around the world are only as good as the Airmen who work in them. Providing essential care in multiple medical roles, Aerospace Medical Service specialists assist doctors and care for patients in a wide range of situations. From administering immunizations to assisting in aeromedical evacuations, these highly skilled professionals supply critical support and are valuable members of any healthcare team.

Aerospace Medical Service specialists perform a wide array of technical nursing duties involving the care and treatment of patients, including immunizations, dialysis and critical care. They assemble, operate, and maintain medical equipment, and they schedule and conduct in-service training on procedures and techniques. They administer medications under the supervision of a physician or nurse, and they perform medical, dental and emergency treatment at deployed locations and remote sites. They also prepare patients for surgery and perform postoperative monitoring, and perform aeromedical evacuation ground or flight duties.

Requirements for this Career Field
No record of emotional instability • Must possess a valid state driver's license • Certification from the National Registry of Emergency Medical Technicians as an emergency medical technician • Normal color vision • Immunization Back-up

Technician qualification • Qualification to perform duties at an isolated location

Relevant Interests & Skills
Natural Science • Health & Medicine

Training Location
Ft. Sam Houston, TX for 98 days.

Related Civilian Careers
Emergency Medical Technician & Paramedic • Firefighter • Fire Inspector • Police Officer • Sheriff & Deputy Sheriffs

Minimum ASVAB
50 in General

Security Clearance
None

Shred-outs
(B) Neurodiagnostic Medical Technician
(C) Independent Duty Medical Technician
(F) Flight and Operational Medical Technician

4N1X1
Surgical Service

It takes a team of professionals to ensure that our Airmen and their families get surgical care when they need it. Responsible for assisting surgeons during operations, Surgical Service specialists ensure that every procedure goes as smoothly as possible. These professionals play an integral role on any healthcare team and perform a wide range of critical tasks, from sterilizing tools and prepping the operating room to helping with anesthesia and assisting with patient care.

Surgical Service specialists assist anesthesia personnel and organize the medical environment in preparation for patient care. They aid surgeons during surgery and prepare and maintain a sterile operating area. They sterilize tools for surgery, and order diagnostic laboratory and radiographic procedures as directed.

Requirements for this Career Field
No record of emotional instability • No limitations for continuous standing

Relevant Interests & Skills
Health & Medicine • Health Technicians & Specialists • Natural Science

Training Location
Ft. Sam Houston, TX for 32 - 46 days.

Related Civilian Careers
Surgical Technician • Cardiovascular Technician • Respiratory Therapy Technician • Veterinary Technician • Dental Assistant • Endoscopy Technician

Minimum ASVAB
44 in General

Security Clearance
None

Shred-outs
(B) Urology
(C) Orthopedics
(D) Otolaryngology

4P0X1
Pharmacy Technician

An integral part of keeping our Airmen and their families healthy happens in the pharmacy. Responsible for interpreting, filling and dispensing prescriptions, Pharmacy specialists work with Pharmacists to help keep their patients healthy. These experts also work directly with patients and providers to ensure that they fully understand their medications in order to keep them healthy and safe from unintended misuse.

Pharmacy Technicians prepare drug orders, confer with patients on questions regarding their medications, and they calculate the amount of ingredients needed to make compound drugs. They develop efficient work methods and operating procedures, conduct periodic inspections of drug storage and usage areas, and they safeguard chemicals, drugs and mild narcotics.

Requirements for this Career Field
Normal color vision • Ability to speak distinctly without speech impediment • Ability to keystroke at a rate of 25 words per minute • Ability to communicate clearly, both orally and in writing.

Relevant Interests & Skills
Natural Science • Health & Medicine • Health Technicians & Specialists • Allied Health

Training Location
Ft. Sam Houston, TX for 62 days.

Related Civilian Careers
Pharmacy Technician • Medical Scientist • Health Specialty Teacher • Nursing Instructor

Minimum ASVAB
44 in General

Security Clearance
None

Shred-outs
None

4R0X1
Diagnostic Imaging

Providing full-service healthcare to every Airman and their family means having specialists available to meet every medical need. It's the job of the Diagnostic Imaging specialists to assist physicians by taking X-rays of the entire body in settings ranging from surgery centers to imaging rooms. These professionals utilize highly sophisticated equipment and an intimate knowledge of human anatomy to help get these images and treat their patients.

Diagnostic Imaging specialists operate various types of imaging equipment to perform radiological exams, they engage with patients to make decisions affecting their diagnosis and care, and they use specialized equipment to perform various procedures and imaging. They also perform equipment quality control checks.

Requirements for this Career Field
Minimum age of 18 years prior to technical training

Relevant Interests & Skills
Natural Science • Health & Medicine • Health Technicians & Specialists • Allied Health • Computers & Computer Science

Training Location
Ft. Sam Houston, TX for 340 - 450 days.

Related Civilian Careers
Diagnostic Medical Sonographer • Nuclear Medicine Technician • Radiologic Technician

Minimum ASVAB
44 in General

Security Clearance
None

Shred-outs
(A) Nuclear Medicine
(B) Diagnostic Medical Sonography
(C) Magnetic Resonance Imaging

4T0X1
Medical Laboratory

In order to provide the best healthcare to our Airmen and their families, it's essential for us to be able to supply them with accurate medical diagnosis. Helping conduct essential tests on body substances, Medical Laboratory specialists have an integral role in providing patients with a proper diagnosis and treatment. The state-of-the-art analysis provided by these experts not only helps prevent and treat disease, but is essential to detecting agents that indicate biological warfare.

Medical Laboratory specialists test and analyze specimens using laboratory techniques, they complete processing of blood for transfusion, and they perform chemical analysis and blood bank duties. They keep lab conditions safe and organized, and they maintain records of all laboratory work performed. They also assist biological warfare officer in developing procedures to detect bacteriological agents.

Requirements for this Career Field
Normal color vision

Relevant Interests & Skills
Natural Science • Health & Medicine • Health Technicians & Specialists • Computers & Computer Science

Training Location
Ft. Sam Houston, TX for 268 days.

Related Civilian Careers
Medical & Clinical Lab Technician • Biological Technician • Cytogenetic Technician • Respiratory Therapy Technician

Minimum ASVAB
62 in General

Security Clearance
None

Shred-outs
None

4T0X2
Histopathology

Providing first-rate medical care often requires specialized examination to occur behind the scenes. Responsible for preparing tissue for examination, Histopathology specialists help with essential diagnosis of the diseased samples. These technicians work in hospital labs performing various duties that range from maintaining laboratory instruments to assisting pathologists to perform autopsies in pursuit of the medical answers needed to treat patients.

Histopathology specialists receive and prepare surgical specimens for tissue diagnosis, they maintain records of all surgical, cytological, and autopsy specimens, and they serve as a technical assistant during autopsies. They evaluate current and new procedures for implementation and effectiveness, and they assist in maintaining accreditation standards.

Requirements for this Career Field
Normal color vision

Relevant Interests & Skills
Natural Science • Health & Medicine • Health Technicians & Specialists • Allied Health

Training Location
Ft. Sam Houston, TX for 100 days.

Related Civilian Careers
Histotechnologist & Histologic Technician • Chemical Technician • Endoscopy Technician • Neurodiagnostic Technician • Medical & Clinical Lab Technician

Minimum ASVAB
44 in General

Security Clearance
None

Shred-outs
None

ENSURING EVERYONE SEES CLEARLY

4V0X1
Ophthalmic

Regardless of job duty, it's essential for each of our Airmen to have good vision. Responsible for performing visual tests and procedures, Optometry specialists assist Optometrists with the treatment of patients. From aiding in the diagnosis of eye disorders to assisting Airmen with aviator contact lenses, these professionals play an integral part in helping patients see better and protect their eyes.

Ophthalmic specialists assist the healthcare provider in the examination and treatment of patients by performing visual tests and procedures. They administer ophthalmic drops and ointments and apply ocular dressings, and they order, fit, and dispense military eyewear. They perform as an ophthalmic surgical assistant and prepare pre- and postoperative patients. They also direct budget and manage ophthalmic activities.

Requirements for this Career Field
Vision correctable to at least 20/30 in either eye • No detectable central scotoma in either eye with best acuity

Relevant Interests & Skills
Natural Science • Health & Medicine

Training Location
Ft. Sam Houston, TX for 53 days.

Related Civilian Careers
Opticians • Wholesale & Retail Buyers • Pharmacy Technician • Medical Assistant • Retail Salesperson

Minimum ASVAB
55 in General

Security Clearance
None

Shred-outs:
(S) - Ophthalmology

Dental Careers (4Y)

The Dental career field provides paraprofessional support in the delivery of dental health care to authorized beneficiaries both in garrison and in a deployed environment. This includes assisting in general dentistry, oral and maxillofacial surgery, prosthodontics, endodontics, periodontics, orthodontics, and pediatric dentistry.

4Y0X1
Dental Assistant

Airmen and their families are posted around the world, and they all receive top-notch dental care. Working alongside dentists, Air Force Dental Assistants help provide patient care in every procedure. Responsible for aiding in every part of the practice from simple exams and taking x-rays to assisting in oral surgery, these specialists ensure that patients remain healthy and comfortable at all times.

Dental Assistants assist Air Force Dentists in the treatment of patients, assist in specialty areas such as oral surgery, periodontics, and endodontics, and they take, develop and mount dental x-rays. They instruct patients in dental health maintenance, and also coordinate patient appointments and maintain dental health records.

Requirements for this Career Field
Normal color vision • Minimum age of 18 years prior to technical training

Relevant Interests & Skills
Natural Science • Health & Medicine • Dentistry

Training Location
Ft. Sam Houston, TX for 48 days.

Related Civilian Careers
Dental Hygienist • Dental Assistant • Radiological Technician • Surgical Technician • Endoscopy Technician • Neurodiagnostic Technician

Minimum ASVAB
44 in General

Security Clearance
None

Shred-outs
(H) Dental Hygienist

4Y0X2
Dental Laboratory

When Airmen need dental work, their needs can sometimes require more complex care. Providing behind-the-scenes expertise, Dental Laboratory specialists assist dentists by crafting and creating custom dental prostheses. These highly skilled experts use the latest tools and techniques and work with dental materials such as acrylic, gypsum and gold to make precision pieces for their patients that they'll utilize for years to come.

Dental Laboratory specialists fabricate and repair dentures, crowns, partial dentures, mouth guards and other types of appliances. They work with a wide variety of dental materials, including metals, resins and porcelain. They also manage dental laboratory equipment and maintain dental laboratory records, and they inspect equipment and perform minor maintenance.

Requirements for this Career Field
Normal color vision

Relevant Interests & Skills
Natural Science • Health & Medicine • Dentistry

Training Location
Ft. Sam Houston, TX for 130 days.

Related Civilian Careers
Dental Laboratory Technician • Electromechanical Equipment Assembler • Photographic Process Worker & Processing Machine Operator

Minimum ASVAB
66 in General

Security Clearance
None

Shred-outs
None

Paralegal Careers (5J)

Paralegals perform legal duties under the supervision of an attorney in compliance with American Bar Association Standards and the Air Force Rules of Professional Conduct.

5J0X1
Paralegal

Just as in the civilian world, it's essential that our Airmen have access to excellent legal services when necessary. Working under the supervision of Judge Advocate Generals (attorneys), Paralegal specialists help provide legal counsel and services to their clients. These legal experts work in a wide range of legal practices doing everything from research and interviews to processing cases and discovery management in order to ensure the law, order and discipline of the Air Force.

Paralegal specialists manage and perform legal functions within statutory guidelines and the Air Force Rules of Professional Conduct. They conduct legal research and make final legal recommendations for the Staff Judge Advocate, and they develop and maintain legal assistance materials and resources for clients. They also provide administrative and litigation support for all judicial and non-judicial matters, and they interview clients and determine eligibility for legal assistance.

Requirements for this Career Field

Ability to communicate effectively in writing • Ability to keyboard at a minimum rate of 25 words per minute • Ability to speak clearly and distinctly • No significant record of emotional instability, personality disorder, or other unresolved mental health concerns • No record of substance abuse, domestic violence, or child abuse • No convictions by a civilian court except for minor traffic violations • Completion of a current National Agency Check, Local Agency Checks and Credit

Relevant Interests & Skills
Law & Enforcement • Operations & Administration

Training Location
Maxwell AFB, AL for 35 days.

Related Civilian Careers
Paralegal • Legal Assistant • Billing, Cost, and Rate Clerk • Bookkeeping, Accounting, and Auditing Clerk • Administrative Assistant

Minimum ASVAB
51 in General

Security Clearance
Secret

Shred-outs
None

Contracting Careers (6C)

The Contracting career field encompasses the purchasing of equipment, supplies, services, and construction through negotiation or formal advertising methods or both This field involves soliciting bids; preparing, processing, awarding, and administering contractual documents; maintaining records of obligations, bid deposits, and miscellaneous purchasing transactions; and providing for contract repair services.

6C0X1
Contracting

As a major purchaser of supplies and services, it is essential that we receive the best value for every dollar spent. Responsible in assisting in the contract process, Contracting specialists follow strict standards and practices to ensure every detail is covered every step of the way. These professionals help prepare, negotiate and award contracts to qualified vendors as well as evaluate their performances to ensure that the money we spend is put to its best possible use.

Contracting specialists obtain data on marketing trends, supply sources and trade information. They analyze prices before preparing an order or contract, and they understand all contract clauses and special provisions. They prepare and send solicitation documents to companies for price quotes, they resolve contract problems, and they buy equipment, supplies, services and construction to support base activities.

Requirements for this Career Field
Ability to communicate effectively in writing • Ability to speak distinctly • Never been convicted by a civilian court of a Category 1, 2, or 3 offense, nor exceeded the accepted number of Category 4 offenses. Category 3 and 4 traffic offenses alone are not disqualifying

Relevant Interests & Skills
Operations & Administration

Training Location
Lackland AFB, TX for 40 days.

Related Civilian Careers
Procurement Clerk • Insurance Adjuster • Tax Examiner & Collector • Bookkeeping, Accounting, and Auditing • Brokerage Clerk

Minimum ASVAB
72 in General

Security Clearance
None

Shred-outs
None

Financial Careers (6F)

The Financial career field involves receiving, disbursing, and accounting for public funds; appropriation and expense, working capital, and real property accounting, including reporting and analyzing costs of programs and operations; formulating, executing, and analyzing financial programs; and examining and verifying all Air Force financial and management operations.

6F0X1
Financial Management and Comptroller

Like any effective organization, the Air Force must work to accomplish its goals with financial responsibility. It's the job of Financial Management and Comptroller specialists to manage the accounting records and systems. From determining the availability of funds to processing the dispersal of payments to performing audits, these experts keep a watchful eye on our financial data to ensure that our funds are being utilized responsibly and efficiently.

Financial Management and Comptroller specialists advise, interact, and coordinate with organizations on financial matters. They determine funds available for procurement action and for accuracy of amounts claimed, and they process financial transactions. They review all accounts for funds concerning operating cost, accounting, payments to vendors and any working capital funds. They also provide customer service and financial analysis for various organizations and vendors, and they perform audits and reviews as required.

Requirements for this Career Field
No record of conviction by a civilian court for offenses involving larceny, robbery, wrongful appropriation, or burglary, or fraud

Relevant Interests & Skills
Operations & Administration

Training Location
Keesler AFB, MS for 57 days.

Related Civilian Careers
Payroll and Timekeeping Clerk • Bill and Account Collectors • Bookkeeping, Accounting, and Auditing Clerk • Receptionist • Insurance Claims Clerk

Minimum ASVAB
57 in General

Security Clearance
None

Shred-outs
None

Appendix One: Mechanical AFSCs

AFSC	Score	AFSC	Score
1A9X1	60	2F0X1	47
1C2X1	55	2M0X2	47
1C7X1	40	2T1X1	40
1P0X1	40	2T2X1	47
2A3X3	47	2T3X1	47
2A3X7	47	2T3X1A	40
2A3X8	47	2T3X1C	40
2A5X1	47	2W0X1	60
2A5X2B	56	2W1X1	60
2A5X2D	51	2W2X1	60
2A5X4	47	3D1X7	55
2A6X1	56	3E0X1	35
2A6X2	47	3E0X2	56
2A6X3	56	3E1X1	47
2A6X4	47	3E2X1	40
2A6X5	56	3E3X1	47
2A6X6	41	3E4X1	47
2A7X1	47	3E8X1	60
2A7X2	42	3P0X1B	35
2A7X3	47	4A2X1	60
2A7X5	47	-----	--

Appendix Two: Administrative AFSCs

AFSC	Score	AFSC	Score
1C0X2	41	2T3X7	41
1C3X1	55	3F0X1	41
1N0X1	64	3F4X1	41
2G0X1	56	3F5X1	47
2S0X1	41	3N1X1	21
2T0X1	35	3N2X1	21
2T2X1	28	5R0X1	35

Appendix Three: General AFSCs

AFSC	Score	AFSC	Score
1A0X1	55	1W0X2	66
1A2X1	57	2F0X1	38
1A8X1	72	2R0X1	55
1A8X2	72	2R1X1	44
1A9X1	57	2S0X1	44
1C1X1	55	2W0X1	57
1C2X1	55	3D0X1	64
1C3X1	67	3D0X2	64 / 54*
1C4X1	49	3D0X3	64 / 54*
1C5X1	55	3D0X4	64 / 54*
1C7X1	50	3E4X3	38
1N1X1	66	3E5X1	49
1N2X1A	72	3E6X1	44
1N2X1C	72 / 67*	3E7X1	38
1N3X1	72	3E8X1	64
1N4X1A	62 / 57*	3E9X1	62
1N4X1B	62	3F1X1	24
1T0X1	55	3H0X2	72
1T2X1	44	3H0X5	72
1U0X1	64	3N1X1	24
1U1X1	64	3N2X1	24
1W0X1	66	3P0X1	33

AFSC	Score	AFSC	Score
3P0X1A	33	4N1X1	44
4A0X1	44	4P0X1	44
4A1X1	44	4R0X1	44
4B0X1	49	4T0X1	62
4C0X1	55	4T0X2	44
4D0X1	44	4V0X1	55
4E0X1	44	4Y0X1	44
4H0X1	44	4Y0X2	66
4J0X2	62 / 49*	5J0X1	51
4J0X2A	49	6C0X1	72
4M0X1	44	6F0X1	57
4N0X1	50	-----	--

(*) Denotes the minimum required score in General as long as a score of 60 or more has been achieved on the Cyber-Test.

Appendix Four: Electrical AFSCs

AFSC	Score	AFSC	Score
1A3X1	70	2A8X2	70
1C6X1	70	2A9X1	70
1C8X3	70	2A9X2	70
1U0X1	54	2A9X3	70
1U1X1	54	2M0X1	70
1W0X1	50	2M0X3	70
1W0X2	50	2P0X1	70
2A0X1	70	2W1X1	45
2A2X1	70	3D1X1	60 / 55*
2A2X2	70	3D1X2	70 / 60*
2A2X3	70	3D1X3	70
2A3X4	70	3D1X7	55
2A3X5	70	3E0X1	35
2A5X3	70	3E0X2	40
2A6X2	28	3E1X1	28
2A6X6	61	3E4X1	28
2A8X1	70	4A2X1	70

(*) Denotes the minimum required score in Electrical as long as a score of 60 or more has been achieved on the Cyber-Test.

Appendix Five: Additional Retraining AFSCs

The AFCSs listed here are only available for those who have previously held, and were trained in an AFSC. Since this book is geared towards an audience looking to join the Air Force for the first time, descriptions of these career paths are not included in this edition, but are listed in this appendix for completeness.

AFSC	Title	MAGE	Score
1A1X1	Flight Engineer	G	57
1A6X1	Flight Attendant	A	28
1B4X1	Cyber Warfare Operations	G	64
1N7X1	Human Intelligence	G	72
1S0X1	Safety	G	55
3D1X4	Spectrum Operations	E	60
3F2X1	Education & Training	G	59
3F3X1	Manpower	G	66
3F4X1	Equal Opportunity	A / G	41 / 44
3G0X1	Air National Guard Strength Management	N/A	N/A
3H0X1	Historian	G	72
5R0X1	Chaplain Assistant	A / G	35 / 44
7S0X1	Special Investigations	G	44

The MAGE column above refers to (M)echanical, (A)dministrative, (G)eneral, and (E)lectrical.

Appendix Six: Special Duty Identifiers (SDI)

The SDIs listed here are only available for those who have previously held, and were trained in an AFSC. Since this book is geared towards an audience looking to join the Air Force for the first time, descriptions of these career paths are not included in this edition, but are listed in this appendix for completeness.

SDI	Title	MAGE	Score
8A100	Career Assistance Advisor	N/A	N/A
8A200	Enlisted Aide	N/A	N/A
8A300	Protocol	N/A	N/A
8B000	Military Training Instructor	N/A	N/A
8B100	Military Training Leader	N/A	N/A
8B200	Academy Military Training NCO	G	49
8C000	Airman & Family Readiness Center Readiness NCO	N/A	N/A
8D100	Language & Culture Advisor	G	60
8F000	First Sergeant	N/A	N/A
8G000	USAF Honor Guard	N/A	N/A
8G100	USAF Honor Guard Manager	N/A	N/A
8H000	Airmen Dorm Leader	G	47
8I000	Superintendent Inspections	N/A	N/A
8P000	Courier	G	44

SDI	Title	MAGE	Score
8P100	Defense Attaché	N/A	N/A
8R000	Enlisted Accessions Recruiter	N/A	N/A
8R200	Second-Tier Recruiter	G	24
8R300	Third-Tier Recruiter	G	24
8S000	Missile Facility Manager	M	40
8T000	Professional Military Education Instructor	N/A	N/A
8T100	Enlisted Professional Military Education Instructional System Designer	N/A	N/A
8U000	Unit Deployment Manager	A	56

The MAGE column above refers to (M)echanical, (A)dministrative, (G)eneral, and (E)lectrical.

Appendix Seven: AFSCs Open to Non-US Citizens

AFSC	AFSC	AFSC
1S0X1	3F4X1	4Y0X1
2S0X1	3G0X1	4Y0X2
2T0X1	3N1X1	5J0X1
2T1X1	3N2X1	5R0X1
2T2X1	4A0X1	6C0X1
2T3X1	4A1X1	6F0X1
2T3X7	4A2X1	8A100
3D1X7	4B0X1	8A200
3E0X1	4C0X1	8B000
3E0X2	4D0X1	8B100
3E1X1	4E0X1	8B200
3E2X1	4H0X1	8C000
3E3X1	4J0X2	8D100
3E4X1	4M0X1	8F000
3E4X3	4N0X1	8H000
3E5X1	4N1X1	8R000
3E6X1	4P0X1	8R200
3F0X1	4R0X1	8R300
3F1X1	4T0X1	8T000
3F2X1	4T0X2	8T100
3F3X1	4V0X1	8U000

Appendix Eight: Air Force Eligibility Standards

Joining the Air Force is a rather simple process, and an Air Force recruiter will guide you through each step along the way. The Air Force maintains high standards among those who are allowed to serve, and most of these standards are within your control. This chapter will help you to make sure that you meet the requirements now, and that you will be well informed to make decisions in the future to maintain your eligibility throughout your Air Force career.

Personal Beliefs

A person with firm fixed personal beliefs, convictions, or religious practices precluding unrestricted duties or assignments; or who received a presidential pardon for draft evasion are ineligible to enlist.

Religious Accommodation

A request for religious accommodation by any pre-accession applicant cannot be granted. Instead, applicants are briefed on Air Force policy and procedures for seeking accommodation. Specifically, applicants are briefed that every airman has the right to request accommodation once they have been accessed into the

Air Force. Religious accommodation requests are reviewed and evaluated on a case-by-case basis at each assignment throughout the airman's career. As such, a religious accommodation may be granted at one assignment but denied at another assignment. Every request is fully considered by the authority; however, if the request is denied the airman will be required to comply with Air Force standards. Following the briefing, the applicant's acknowledgment of the Air Force policy regarding accommodation requests will be recorded and maintained as part of the accession application.

Drug Use

A current or history of alcohol dependence, drug dependence, alcohol abuse, or other drug abuse is incompatible with military life and does not meet military standards. Any person found to be intoxicated or under the influence of alcohol or drugs during the enlistment process will be ineligible. All applicants will complete an AF Form 2030, *USAF Drug and Alcohol Abuse Certificate.* Any drug use after signing this form will make the applicant ineligible for enlistment or waiver consideration. Applicants who refuse to be drug tested will not be enlisted. Individuals who test positive on the Drug and Alcohol test will be permanently barred from the Air Force.

The Air Force will not disqualify persons due to alcohol addiction if the persons were known to be or have been addicted to alcohol provide documentation indicating successful completion of rehabilitation program and have maintained sobriety for a minimum of two years.

Height and Weight Requirements

The Air Force maintains strict height and weight requirements. All applicants must meet a weight requirement based on their height. Height is in inches and maximum weight is in pounds.

Height	Max Weight	Height	Max Weight
58	131	70	191
59	136	71	197
60	141	72	202
61	145	73	208
62	150	74	214
63	155	75	220
64	160	76	225
65	165	77	231
66	170	78	237
67	175	79	244
68	180	80	250
69	186	--	---

Medical Standards

The Department of Defense has set forth guidelines and requirements for basic medical standards for enlistment, appointment, and induction into the Armed Forces of the United States under DoDI 6130.03. Under this authority are medical conditions and physical defects that are causes for rejection for military service. This instruction is quite extensive and in-depth, so if you have any questions regarding what may disqualify you medically from serving, look this policy up on the internet.

Age

A Non-Prior Service applicant must be at least 17 years old, but not reached the age of 40 on his Date of Enlistment. Applicants that have not turned 18 years of age must have parental or guardian consent. Parental or guardian consent is not required for an emancipated 17 year old; however, an emancipated 17 year old must have an approved waiver. Parental or guardian consent is not required for a married 17 year old applicant.

A Prior Service applicant uses an adjusted age. To calculate the adjusted age, subtract the applicants years of satisfactory service, from the applicants age.

The Air Force maintains strict height and weight requirements. All applicants must meet a weight requirement based on their height. Height is in inches and maximum weight is in pounds.

Citizenship Standards

Any Non-Prior Service (NPS) applicant must be a United States (US) citizen, or an alien lawfully admitted into the US for permanent residence. An NPS may be a US National born in American Samoa or Swains Island, Palau, or Foreign national citizen of the Federated States of Micronesia or the Republic of the Marshall Islands.

American Indians born in Canada are considered immigrant aliens and must present a birth certificate. These applicants may enlist, but will not receive a security clearance until they become a US citizen.

Individuals that have dual citizenship with another country and the US, will not be placed into an Air Force Specialty Code listed as "Open to non-US citizens".

If the applicant formerly served in the Peace Corps, they must enlist in an Air Force Specialty other than intelligence.

A Prior Service applicant that requires completion of a DD Form 4, *Enlistment/Reenlistment Document Armed Forces of the United States*, must be a US Citizen. (Citizens of the Northern Mariana Islands are considered citizens of the US and not US Nationals.)

Dependency Requirements

Service in the United States Air Force entails potential sacrifice in the form of frequent training periods, duty away from family members in the event of deployments, the demands of shift work, and 24-hour availability to accomplish the mission.

The Air Force defines a family member as:
- A spouse of an applicant.
- An unmarried adopted child or an unmarried step-child under the age of 18 living with the applicant.
- An unmarried biological child of the applicant under the age of 18.
- Any person living with the applicant who is, by law or in fact, dependent upon the applicant for support, or who is not living with the applicant and is dependent upon the applicant for over one-half of his or her support.

- For male applicants only, the spouse's unborn child, one the applicant claims, or a court order determines to be his.

Applicants are ineligible for enlistment if they are married and have legal or physical custody of:
- More than two dependents under the age of 18, or
- More than two dependents over 18 and lives with the applicant, or does not live with them and the applicant provides over one-half of his or her support, or
- A combination of more than two dependents as outlined above.

Applicants are ineligible for enlistment if they are unmarried and have legal or physical custody of:
- Any dependents under the age of 18, or
- Any dependents over 18 and lives with the applicant, or does not live with them and the applicant provides over one-half of his or her support

Waivers or determination for ineligible applicants may be granted for particularly promising entrants as defined by the waiver authority.

Prior service applicants accessing in the pay grade of E-4 or higher and are otherwise qualified for service do not need to complete a Dependency Waiver/Determination.

Applicants who have dependents must complete an AF Form 357, Family Care Certification prior to enlistment.

Education Requirements

Applicants must be a high school graduate, covered graduate (non-traditional high school graduate), or alternate credential holder, to include holder of General Education Development (GED), or completion of one semester of college credit (15 semester hours or 22.5 quarter hours). High school seniors and covered graduates in their senior year may start the enlistment process with a statement from school officials stating he or she has or will obtain sufficient acceptable credits to be awarded a high school diploma.

High School Graduates and Covered Graduates must obtain an Armed Forces Qualification Test (AFQT) score of 36 or higher on the ASVAB. Alternate Credential Holders must obtain an AFQT score of 50 or higher on the ASVAB. Non-graduates and non-alternate credential holders must obtain an AFQT score of 65 or higher on the ASVAB.

Each year the Air Force must ensure that 95% of all enlistees are high school graduates or covered graduates that have an AFQT score of 36 or higher, and that 60% of all enlistees must have a score of 50 or higher on the AFQT.

Body Alteration/Modification

Intentional alterations and/or modifications to a members body that result in a visible, physical effect that disfigures, deforms or otherwise detracts from a professional military image are prohibited. Examples include tongue splitting or forking, acquiring visible, disfiguring skin implants, and gouging.

Prior Service Applicants

A Prior Service applicant must have completed an approved basic military training course and must have completed 84 days or more of Initial Active Duty Training. Air Force applicants who were separated from Basic Military Training due to pregnancy are given priority to re-enter training as soon as medically qualified without having to re-compete and must meet all other qualifications.

If currently serving in the US Armed Forces, active or reserve, member must obtain a signed conditional release prior to enlistment.

Prior Service applicants discharged solely under 10 USC § 654, commonly known as "Don't Ask, Don't Tell" or "DADT" and its implementing regulations may apply to reenter the Air Force. These applicants are evaluated according to the same criteria and requirements applicable to all Prior Service members seeking reentry into the Air Force.

Prior Service applicants are ineligible if they previously served in another country's armed forces, or if they previously received any discharge other than honorable or uncharacterized discharge or were separated for cause for the last period of service; or whose discharge was due to Fitness Failure, Inaptitude, Fraud, Misconduct, or Unsuitability. They are also ineligible if they were eliminated from an officer candidate training program based on punitive or administrative actions involving defective character traits, unsuitability, alcohol, or drug abuse. Prior Service applicants are also ineligible if they currently hold a commission or warrant in any US Armed Forces or if they are a student of any US military academy.

Tattoos, Brands, Body Markings

Tattoos, brands, or body markings anywhere on the body that are obscene, commonly associated with gangs, extremist, and/or supremacist organizations, or that advocate sexual, racial, ethnic, or religious discrimination are prohibited in and out of uniform.

Excessive tattoos, brands, or body markings will not be exposed or visible while wearing any or all uniform combinations, except the physical training uniform. "Excessive" is defined as any tattoos, brands, or body markings that exceed ¼ or 25% of the exposed body part and are readily visible when wearing any/all uniform combinations. "Exposed body part" is defined as the total area, to include front, sides, and back of a limb or other body part protruding from a uniform item. Tattoos, brands, or markings are prohibited above the collarbone.

Morals & Legal Issues

The purpose of the following enlistment standards are to minimize entrance of persons who are likely to become disciplinary cases, security risks, or who are likely to disrupt good order, morale, and discipline. The Air Force is responsible for the defense of the Nation and should not be viewed as a source of rehabilitation for those who have not subscribed to the legal and moral stands of society at-large.

An applicant is ineligible to enlist is they have unpaid fines, or are under any form of judicial restraint such as bond, probation, imprisonment, or parole. An applicant is not eligible to begin enlistment processing for 90 days following termination of parole, probation, suspended sentence, or any period of confinement for a conviction, except for suspended sentences for minor traffic offenses and completion of community service.

A conviction of one or more of the following offenses is disqualifying for entry into the Air Force, without an approved Waiver:

- Adultery
- Aggravated assault, fighting, or battery
- Aggravated sexual contact or Abusive Sexual Contact
- Arson
- Attempt to commit a felony
- Breaking and entering a vehicle
- Breaking and entering with intent to commit a felony
- Bribery
- Burglary
- Carjacking
- Carnal knowledge of a child
- Carrying concealed weapon
- Carrying of a weapon on school grounds
- Check worthless, making or uttering, with intent to defraud or deceive (over $500)
- Child abuse
- Child pornography
- Concealment or failure to report a felony
- Conspiring to commit a felony
- Conspiring to commit a misdemeanor
- Contributing to the delinquency of a minor
- Crimes against the family; contempt of court
- Criminal libel

- Criminal mischief
- Criminal trespass
- Desecration of grave
- Discharging a firearm through carelessness or within municipal limits
- Domestic battery
- Draft evasion
- Drunk in public
- DUI/DWUI/DWI
- Embezzlement
- Extortion
- Failure to appear, contempt of court
- Failure to stop and render aid after accident
- Forgery
- Forcible pandering
- Grand larceny, larceny, shoplifting, petty larceny, theft, or petty theft of stolen goods
- Grand theft auto
- Hate crimes
- Housebreaking
- Illegal and/or fraudulent use of a credit card, bank card, or automated card
- Indecent acts or liberties with a child; molestation
- Indecent assault
- Indecent exposure
- Indecent, insulting, or obscene language communicated directly or by telephone or any electronic method
- Indecent viewing, visual recording or broadcasting
- Involuntary manslaughter
- Kidnapping or abduction

- Killing a domestic animal
- Larceny, shoplifting or conversion
- Leaving the scene of accident, when considered hit and run
- Lewd, licentious or lascivious behavior
- Liquor or alcoholic beverages: unlawful manufacture, sale, possession, or consumption in a public place
- Looting
- Mail or electronic emission matters: abstracting, destroying, obstructing, opening, secreting, stealing, or taking
- Mailbox destruction
- Mailing, to include e-mail, of obscene or indecent matter
- Maiming or disfiguring
- Malicious mischief
- Manslaughter
- Murder
- Narcotics or habit-forming drugs: wrongful possession or use (marijuana not included)
- Negligent or vehicular manslaughter
- Other misconduct offenses not specifically listed
- Pandering
- Perjury or subordination of perjury
- Possession of marijuana or drug paraphernalia
- Possession or intent to use materials in a manner to make a bomb or explosive device to cause bodily harm or destruction of property
- Possession/carrying of weapon on school grounds
- Prostitution or solicitation for prostitution
- Public record; altering, concealing, destroying, mutilating, obliterating, or removing

- Rape, sexual abuse, sexual assault, criminal sexual abuse, incest, or other sex crimes
- Reckless endangerment
- Reckless, careless or imprudent driving
- Removing property from public grounds
- Removing property under lien
- Resisting, fleeing or eluding arrest
- Riot
- Robbery, to include armed
- Sale, distribution, or trafficking of cannabis (marijuana) or any other controlled substance (including intent)
- Sedition or soliciting to commit sedition
- Selling or leasing weapons
- Sexual harassment
- Shooting from highway
- Slander
- Sodomy
- Stalking
- Stolen property, knowingly received
- Terroristic threats including bomb threats
- Throwing rocks on a highway; throwing missiles at sporting events; throwing objects at vehicles
- Unlawful carrying of firearms or carrying concealed firearm
- Unlawful or illegal entry
- Use of telephone, internet, or other electronic means to abuse, annoy, harass, threaten, or torment another
- Vandalism, defacing or injuring property ($500+ fine or confinement)
- Violation of civil rights

- Willfully discharging firearm so as to endanger life; shooting in public
- Wrongful appropriation of a motor vehicle, joyriding, or driving without the owner's consent

Two convictions in the last three years or three or more convictions in a lifetime of the following offenses is disqualifying for entry into the Air Force, without an approved Waiver:

- Altered driver's license or identification
- Assault (simple assault with fine of $500 or less an no confinement
- Check worthless, making or uttering, with intent to defraud or deceive (less than $500)
- Check: $250 or less, insufficient funds, or worthless
- Committing or creating a nuisance
- Curfew violation
- Damaging road signs
- Disorderly conduct; creating disturbance; boisterous conduct
- Disturbing the peace
- Drinking alcoholic beverages on public transportation
- Dumping refuse near highway
- Failure to appear (other than traffic, comply with judgment, or answer or disobey summons)
- Failure to appear, contempt of court (all offenses except felony proceedings)
- Fare/toll evasion
- Fighting, participating in a brawl
- Harassment, menacing or stalking (non-sexual)

- Illegal betting or gambling: operating illegal handbook, raffle, lottery, or punch board; cockfighting
- Jumping turnstile
- Littering
- Loitering
- Operating a motor vehicle after consumption of less than legal limit of alcohol, while under legal drinking age
- Other non-traffic offenses not specifically listed
- Poaching
- Possession of indecent publications or pictures (other than child pornography)
- Purchase, possession, or consumption of tobacco/alcoholic beverages by a minor
- Reckless, careless or imprudent driving
- Robbing an orchard
- Shoplifting, larceny, petty larceny, theft, or petty theft (committed under age 14 and stolen goods valued at $50 or less
- Throwing glass or other material in roadway
- Trespass on property (non-criminal/simple)
- Unlawful assembly
- Unlawful use of long distance telephone calling card
- Using or wearing unlawful emblem and/or identification
- Vagrancy
- Vandalism, defacing or injuring property ($500 or less and no confinement)
- Violation of fireworks law
- Violation of fish and game laws
- Violation of leash laws
- Violation of probation

Six or more convictions in a 365-day period in the last three years of the following is disqualifying for entry into the Air Force, without an approved Waiver:

- Bicycle ordinance violation
- Blocking or retarding traffic
- Contempt of court for minor traffic offenses
- Crossing yellow line; driving left of center
- Disobeying traffic lights, signs, or signals
- Driving on shoulder
- Driving uninsured vehicle
- Driving with blocked or impaired vision/tinted windows
- Driving with expired plates or without plates
- Driving with suspended or revoked license or never issued a license
- Driving without license in possession
- Driving without registration or with improper registration
- Driving wrong way on one-way street
- Failure to appear for traffic violations
- Failure to comply with officer's directive
- Failure to have vehicle under control
- Failure to signal
- Failure to stop or yield to pedestrian
- Failure to submit report after accident
- Failure to yield right-of-way
- Faulty equipment, such as defective exhaust, horn, lights, mirror, muffler, signal device, steering device, tail pipe or windshield wipers
- Following too closely

- Hitchhiking
- Improper backing, such as backing into intersection or highway, backing on expressway, or backing over crosswalk
- Improper blowing of horn
- Improper passing (passing on right, passing in no-passing zone, passing stopped school bus, or passing pedestrian in crosswalk)
- Improper turn
- Invalid or unofficial inspection sticker, failure to display inspection sticker
- Jaywalking
- Leaving key in ignition
- Leaving the scene of accident (when not hit and run)
- License plates improperly displayed or not displayed
- Operating overloaded vehicle
- Other traffic offenses not specifically listed
- Racing, dragging, or contest for speed
- Seatbelt and/or child restraint violation
- Skateboard, roller skate, or inline skating violation
- Speeding
- Spilling load on highway
- Spinning wheels, improper start, zigzagging, or weaving in traffic
- Violation of noise control ordinance

www.ingramcontent.com/pod-product-compliance
Lightning Source LLC
Chambersburg PA
CBHW071619220526
45469CB00002B/408